projected cities

STEPHEN BARBER

REAKTION BOOKS

Reaktion Books Ltd
79 Farringdon Road
London EC1M 3JU

www.reaktionbooks.co.uk

First published 2002

Printed and bound in Great Britain by Cromwell Press, Trowbridge, Wiltshire

British Library Cataloguing in Publication Data

Barber, Stephen, 1961 –
    Projected Cities: Cinema and Urban Space. – (Locations)
    1. Cities and towns in motion pictures
    I. Title
    791.4'3621732

ISBN 1 86189 127 X

contents

introduction

The rapport between cinema and urban space has formed a determining force, for over a century, behind the ways in which history and the human body have been visualized and mediated. This book surveys the intricate connections between film images and cities, with a particular focus on the urban cinema cultures of Europe and Japan – the two vital, interconnected visual arenas in the exploration of imageries of the contemporary city, and also the locations in which film has exhaustively captured periods of urban upheaval and transformation throughout cinema's history. In its interaction with the city, film carries a multiplicity of means through which to reveal elements of corporeal, cultural, architectural, historical and social forms, as well as to project the preoccupations with memory, death and the origins of the image that crucially interlock cinema with urban space. This book emphasizes film imageries of cities at moments of turmoil and experimentation, whether in the physical and sensory dimensions of the city or on its exterior surfaces. The book finally assesses the impact of contemporary media culture on the status of film, on cinema spaces and on the visual rendering of the contemporary moment in the digital city.

Part I examines the origins of the film city, looking at the formative work in Europe of often occluded figures in the innovation of urban images such as Louis Le Prince in England and the Skladanowsky Brothers in Germany. The depiction of human bodies against urban space, and the attraction of spectators for film images, formed fundamental components in those first probings of urban cinema. Subsequent experiments, especially those conducted in the USSR and France during the second half of the 1920s by such film-makers as Dziga Vertov and the Surrealists, concentrated on the representation of the forms of the city in juxtaposition with the dynamics of sensory perception; the body acquired and lost its pre-eminence as the point of intersection between the image and the city. Throughout the first half of the twentieth century, film was often used as a medium both for portraying and for precipitating urban revolution, and, contrarily, for the imposition of oppressive power structures in the city. At the end of the Second World War, across Europe, film imageries of destroyed cities proved seminal to the ways in which urban space would be imagined and formulated.

In Part II, the compelling issues of urban space in European cinema, after 1945, are shown to be the exposure by film of the city's historical and visual shifts, and the implications of those shifts for the forms of perception and of the human body. Above all, film developed into the foremost medium of visual memory, comprising the instrument by which its often corrosive traces became engrained in urban space. Film explored the ways in which the city's inhabitants responded to vast changes in visual technologies, to architectural transmutations and to destabilizing flux within essential urban structures; film-makers became preoccupied with exile and with the creation of peripheral spaces within the city, spaces of both social subjugation and dissident opposition. In films from the 1960s on, urban space is often perceived, with both nostalgia and ferocity, as being lost or derelict, and the idea of Europe becomes that of a ruined zone, subject to internal disintegration or to supplantation by external presences. After 1989, the visual saturation of corporate culture over the surfaces of the city possesses renewed repercussions for cinema and for its capacity to sustain an interrogation of urban and corporeal existence.

Part III parallels the upheaval in European urban space across the post-war decades with that taking place in Japan over the same period. Japanese post-war urban space, too, emerged from imageries of devastated cities, which configured its development over the subsequent decades, pre-eminently in the vast reconstruction of Tokyo into sectors structured around sex, work and revolt, each area incisively examined by the medium of cinema. The cinematic oscillation between Europe and Japan is particularly evident in incursions by European film-makers (such as Andrey Tarkovsky and Chris Marker) into Japan, layering their own preoccupations over Tokyo's incandescent cityscapes and conducting explorations into both European and Japanese urban forms and obsessions. The violent uproar of Tokyo in its late-1960s riots, closely mapped and exacerbated in its sexual and revolutionary dimensions by such film-makers as Toshio Matsumoto and Koji Wakamatsu, interconnects with insurgent film imageries of the same era from Paris and other European cities. In the visual convulsions of the contemporary Japanese city, densely traversed by film images of corporeal mutation, technological mishap and incipient urban calamity, the forms of European cities are also tangibly discernible.

In the final part of the book, the contemporary city's relationship to film and to the vanishing spaces of cinema is at issue; the often elusive manifestations of digital culture, via the media of rapidly surpassed urban screens and surfaces, function in an opposed dimension to film and to the spaces of cinematic projection. In this context, the 'digital' indicates the entirety of the transitory but engulfing visual media of technological and corporate culture – forming a powerful urban reality, or irreality, that constrictively encompasses the entire city and every kind of perception and corporeal experience within it, including the rapport between cinema and its urban spectator. In order to gauge the status and endurance of cinema within urban space, I made an oblique journey across the cinematic landscape of Europe, from Tallinn to Lisbon, exploring the diverse forms of cinemas often held in tension within the digital city's surrounding façades. Pornography proved to be an obstinate means of survival for the medium of film. The intimate rapport between digital culture and film culture pivots on a fundamental mismatch, the contradictions of which are probed in the work of urban film-makers operating simultaneously, often ambivalently, in digital media. All of the past and present traces of urban images are collected into the inexhaustible depository of the city's digital archives, which disclose the essential fragility of visual and corporate cultures. The book closes with an examination of the matters of malfunction and corporeal disappearance in the digital city, and their connections to the future forms of cinema.

Contemporary American cinema is beyond the remit of this book, as is the already well-documented history of Hollywood cinema and the international supremacy of its urban representations. That once vibrant power now shows marked signs of irremediable exhaustion, the industrial structure driving it having been overtaken by a new kind of media power that is far too restive and contrary to inhabit the inert film cities of Hollywood's history. In the contemporary urban arena, that cinema constitutes a diminishing presence, primarily formed of void digital effects and endless repetition, and channelled away into the cellular spaces of the anti-cinematic multiplexes that extend right across Europe's innumerable suburban retail complexes. In many ways, the volatile contemporary culture of Japan and the intricate historical transformations of Europe now provide far more revealing insights into the vital dynamics of urban and cinematic spaces.

1 the origins of the film city

Film began with a scattering of gesturing ghosts, of human bodies walking city streets, within the encompassing outlines of bridges, hotels and warehouses, under polluted industrial skies. The first incendiary spark of the film image – extending across almost every country in the world, around the end of the nineteenth century – propelled forward a history of the body that remains inescapably locked into the history of the city.

The film city forms an entangled matter of image and language, of life and death. It incessantly takes on and discards its multiple figures and manifestations, and, through to its last monochrome nuance or lurid pixel, its vital axis lies in contradiction – every one of the aims and strategies of the film city's innumerable directors has been contested and refused, from the first moments of cinematic imagery. The film city's texture comprises an unsteady amalgam of sexual and corporeal traces, of illuminations and darknesses, of architectural ambitions and their cancellation, and of sudden movements between revolution and stasis. As a result, the film city is containable only in an open book of death and origins, constructed from urban fragments that slip into freefall – in the hidden cracks in celluloid and digital images – so as to conjure the aberrant code of language which can itself perversely originate the essential visual compulsions and sensations of the projected or destroyed film city.

The passage from the photographic to the filmic to the digital image carries its own aberrance and contradictory reversals, which annul any sense of a linear history of cinema. The film image defined itself throughout its early decades via the construction of an aura of originality and uniqueness – in the form of irreplicable visual projections of human and urban forms, often in grandiose combat with one another – but the industrial medium of cinema intractably based itself instead on principles of infinite reproduction: of celluloid film prints, of cinema audiences and even of film-narrative forms. The digital image (as the definitive technological real-ization of this desire for endless reproduction) in effect careers backwards in film history, into the time zone before that of cinema's original images, since the digital image's instantly redundant forms – surpassed and eroded by the incessantly mutating corporate demands that engender them – possess a fundamental and extreme archaism. And, in its multiple births and rebirths, cinema's history ultimately conveys a harsh and conflictual set of beginnings to its film cities. The digital image of the city lacks entirely the raw irregularities through which the original film images of urban life sustained their crucial force of respiration. Cinema history itself was born in negation and cancellation, both of its own forms and of the innumerable pre-filmic experiments (such as the Phantasmagoria, the Ergascopia and the Pantascopia) which proliferated in such urban environments as Paris and London in the early and middle decades of the nineteenth century. All visual obsessions cohere, however ephemerally, into particular forms, which then crack open once again. The history of cinema comprises only one variant of an all-encompassing, multiple history of the potential image, just as each city forms a single, momentary variant of the relentless processes of urban transformation.

The cities at the origins of European cinema are strange Edens, already contaminated in the first illumination of their urban matter: the soot-blackened bridge over the River Aire in Louis Le Prince's experimental images taken in the industrial city of Leeds in 1888; the rooftops of the Pankow district of Berlin in images captured by the Skladanowsky Brothers with the aim of infusing cinema for the first time with the spectacular magic of popular public performance; and the imposing tenements, advertising screens and factory buildings of Lyons, shot from trains, in the Lumière Brothers' vast project of collecting their city's visual components on film. The inhabitants of such cities who were captured, often by chance, in those first images became the primitive corporeal figures of cinema, in a parallel way to that in which – in those final years of the nineteenth century – certain oblivious populations such as the rural inhabitants of Romania or the Aran Islanders of western Ireland were being depicted as Europe's archetypal 'primitive' peoples. Cinema itself, in its years of origin, was often denounced as a 'primitive' or crass medium; in a different register, film history since the 1970s has deliberated over the 'primitive' status of early cinema and its strategies. However, the adroit power struggles for control over the technology of film, and over the urban audiences that it enthralled, quickly became sophisticated as the cinema industry assembled its fragile apparition of aesthetic prestige. In order to secure cinema's status as both art form and mass entertainment product, film's profuse origins were rapidly reinvented as a heroic, mythic achievement, with its unified focus in the work of a few revered pioneers. But cinema and its origins never entirely succeeded in attaching themselves securely to the already unstable forms of early twentieth-century art. And the caustic approach often levelled in contemporary visual cultures towards the sense of a definitive power in images forms yet another reversal for the tenuous prestige accorded to cinema's original images in film history.

In the 1960s, the American film-maker Kenneth Anger often looked back nostalgically to the moment of cinema's origins as a 'black day for mankind', with the medium of film seen as inflicting a literally devilish malediction on humanity, while simultaneously raising the exhilarating creative potential for unrest, turmoil and even revolution. In Europe, the origins of cinema released exactly such a volatile upheaval into the visual perception of cities by their inhabitants. Throughout the first half of the twentieth century, cities became transformed and even brought into existence through the impetus and movement of film images, viewed collectively in the form of exhortative newsreels and feature films within crowded cinema spaces; at the same time, cities reached a point of crisis, and even were abandoned or destroyed, through the impact of film images on urban populations. The torn cities of revolutionary Europe at the end of the First World War, the industrial cities around the far edges of Siberia and the terminated locales of warfare in 1945 all became defined (and in some cases were invented) directly by the medium of the film image. That image powerfully recast the rapport between human vision and the space of the city, according absolute pre-eminence to the future work of the eye. Cinema is the medium that taught the sensory values of speed and intensity to human vision: even the enormous distance extending from the everyday images of life on the city streets in Louis Le Prince's 1888 film to the catastrophic zero-point of Europe's 1945 emptied cities, their utter desolation minutely rendered on film, can be scanned in one rapid eye movement.

The seminal film image forms an exploration of the city designed to capture the maximum intensity of urban life and its actions. The very first work in the history of cinema comprises an image of the city that is imbued with corporeal gestures and urban surfaces together with intimations of death and loss.

In October 1888, the French-born inventor Louis Le Prince positioned his experimental film camera in the window of a tools workshop overlooking the south-east corner of Leeds Bridge, at the busiest moment of the day, and filmed a sequence showing human figures, horse-drawn carriages and carts traversing the river bridge in hazy autumn sunlight. He had selected that moment and site in order to saturate the image with the greatest possible accumulation of human movement. On the far side of the bridge, the smog-encrusted walls of substantial Victorian hotels and warehouses, each façade containing its own unexposed content of human figures, occupied the upper half of the image. The bodies crossing the bridge, unaware of the film being made, were caught in their intricate performance of the originating gestures of cinema. A man wipes his nose; a woman carries a parcel; two men in discussion lean over a parapet; another man politely touches his hat as a woman passes. All of the elements capable of launching an intricate fiction film narrative are already prepared in those banal, scattered gestures. And even within the concentrated temporal span of the film sequence, at the high point of the day's traffic across the bridge, those human figures succeed in sending forth a certain nonchalance: the body's time drifts infinitely. After only three seconds, the film is over.

Although the urban location for Le Prince's film remains tenaciously identical in the contemporary city (all that has changed over twelve decades has been that the surface layer of industrial dirt has been removed from the buildings), every physical gesture that had been enacted on the bridge, and embedded within the film image, vanished instantly. And the surrounding world that had existed at that first cut into time of the film image would shatter, falling apart ever more calamitously as time moved further on and outwards from the image's few impenetrable moments. Le Prince's images initiated the capacity of film, throughout its history, to transfuse to its spectators a compacted charge of nostalgia for the momentary apparitions of cities or human bodies whose forms were just about to disappear forever, fatally engulfed either by conflicts and revolutions or by technological transformations. Le Prince – who had decided to base his research in the thriving industrial city of Leeds after developing the technological basis of his inventions while working as a wallpaper-printing engineer in New York – never found the resources necessary to project his films to audiences, and he moved desperately between France, England and the US in his attempts to engage financial backers in his experiments. During that period, international disputes over the ownership of the technologies of cinema began. Two years after making the original city film in Leeds, Le Prince abruptly disappeared without trace while travelling by train – together with his cameras and projectors – between Dijon and Paris, on 16 September 1890, in the first unsolvable mystery of cinema history. His film of Leeds Bridge remained preserved for 40 years or so, then itself disappeared; a hundred years on from its making, it could only be digitally re-animated from photographs taken in the 1930s of the original images, in an alliance of three conflictual visual media.

As well as seizing, for the first time, the essential banality of everyday human gestures in city streets, Le Prince also became the first film-maker to capture images prescient of death. In the same month as he shot his film of Leeds Bridge, he filmed a sequence in the same city of his elderly mother-in-law dancing, in the garden of her house in the suburban district of Roundhay, ten days before her death. In every film image, the capturing of the body intimates a simultaneous loss of corporeal existence; the immediacy of the image insistently counters sensations of presence with loss. The space of the city itself imbues the film image with an opposed dimension: the city adroitly negotiates and enforces its own mass within the image, applying intricate pressure around the human forms which that image holds. But, once the image has been fixed, its residue in urban space abruptly becomes vulnerable to erasure or alteration – the city is subject to the intrusive power of capricious elements beyond its own domain, in the form of the great upheavals that incessantly amend cities' faces. The innumerable disparities and enigmas that comprise the gap between the contemporary city and its filmed surfaces form the vital core in every human obsession with filmic urban space. But in Le Prince's very first film image of the city, no such disparity occurs, and an outlandish simultaneity arises between the moment of the film city's origin and its contemporary form, thereby summarily closing the gap between film and city. Only the ephemeral traces and memories of the human body have vanished.

Louis Le Prince's films of the city occupy a unique space of flux between invention and death. In his own inexplicable vanishing, he imparted to film history its originating figure of corporeal disappearance – a figure prophetic both for the contemporary impact of digital media on cinema and for the status of the human body within the city's infinitely hazardous arena. Le Prince's often supplanted position within cinema history alternates between utter oblivion and oblique re-instatement, and coheres only within the surviving fragments of his initiatory images of the film city and its gesturing human forms.

In the city-film images of the Skladanowsky Brothers, the rooftops of Berlin's Pankow and Prenzlauer Berg districts stretch outwards across the lower part of the frame, with industrial chimneys and church steeples occasionally punctuating the relentless urban sprawl of factory workers' tenements. While one of the two brothers, Max, operated his film camera, the Bioskop, the other brother, Emil, performed a maladroit dance of bizarrely outstretched arms and legs, facing the lens with a grin and holding his hat high in the air: an aberrant gesture of elation within the framework of those decrepit urban districts, habitually defined by the endlessly repeated gestures of manual labour. Behind the figure in movement of Emil Skladanowsky, a vacant sky occupies the remainder of the frame. Inside the camera, designed to Max Skladanowsky's idiosyncratic specifications, the film jolted from image to image, its perforations having been incised by hand into the celluloid by the film-maker. The image of the human body in the city subsists for a few moments longer than in Le Prince's film, then it too cuts off abruptly, and the body dematerializes. Max Skladanowsky retrospectively provided a date for his images of Berlin, filmed from the roof of a building in the Schön-hauser Allee – 20 August 1892 – although this mythical date may have been as spontaneously invented as his brother's dance on the rooftop overlooking the city. Almost four years had passed since Le Prince's seminal images of the inhabi-tants and urban surfaces of Leeds. In those years, the film cities and populations of Europe had lain dormant, awaiting their next visual resuscitation.

The Skladanowsky Brothers – they hold their place in cinema history as equal collaborators, although it seems clear that Max conducted all of the gruelling work of invention, while the less technologically adept Emil performed the more erratic work of infusing vivid movement into their film images – had begun their visual experiments over a decade earlier, at the end of the 1870s, while demonstrating a variant of one of the innumerable pre-cinema spectacles, the Nebula, to Berlin's novelty-avid population. During that period, the city existed in a state of almost delirious expan-sion and desire for entertainment, as its sudden industrial ascendancy spread its raw, crammed tenement suburbs outwards from the centre. The Nebula spectacle, shown in popular entertainment halls, employed multiple image sources and cacophonies in order to project awesome representations of destroyed cities: they veered disturbingly in and out of focus, suffering multiple catastrophes that ranged from earthquakes to firestorms. The success of the Nebula – undoubtedly more immediate in its compounded sensorial impact than many contemporary digital-image installations with identical strategies – gradually led the Skladanowsky Brothers to envisage presenting their own experimental film images to public audiences.

On 1 November 1895, at the Wintergarten hall in Berlin (a multi-purpose entertainment venue capable of hosting such popular spectacles as acrobatics, wrestling and erotic cabarets, in addition to innovations in the development of the film image), the Skladanowsky Brothers held the first-ever screening of films for a public audience. Their programme lasted for around fifteen minutes and included footage of a boxing kangaroo and of children's folk dances, alongside a number of films of the urban landscapes of Berlin which Max Skladanowsky had filmed especially for the event over the preceding months. The screening's reception proved to be enthusiastic – although most early audiences viewed the images presented to them as flat, monochrome hallucinations of stilted motion, in contrast with the more engulfing spectacles of pre-cinema media. As well as instigating film spectatorship, the Skladanowsky Brothers initiated one further essential component of cinema: the first paying customer entering their Wintergarten screening served unwittingly to activate the financial regime of the cinema industry, thereby irreparably determining the future course of film.

During its first year, cinema projection remained an almost entirely urban phenomenon, with the many inventors of the diverse technologies touring the grand theatres and cafés of the European capitals, their breakneck schedules determined by heated rivalries. Later, films would also be shown to rural audiences, in improvised venues such as barns and stables, with often incendiary results (the first projectors proved notoriously combustible, and early film history is constellated with accounts of audiences fleeing burning cinema spaces). As well as providing a technological and sensory initiation, those rural screenings jolted their audiences with a first vision of the city, as both a potentially dangerous and an alluring destination. During the span of only two months, the fragile position of the Skladanowsky Brothers in film history shifted from one of innovation to one of archaism and incipient oblivion; on 29 December 1895, they travelled to Paris to present their film spectacle at the Folies Bergère, but arrived to discover that their French rivals, the Lumière Brothers, had held their own first public cinema event in the city on the previous day, thereby instantly cornering the Parisian market and necessitating the cancellation of the Skladanowsky Brothers' spectacle. After intermittently touring Northern European cities over the next year in the face of increasingly ferocious competition, the Skladanowsky Brothers abruptly retired from cinema exhibition in 1897 while it was still only in the initial stages of its expansion. Returning home to Berlin, they largely abandoned their inventions and made their living in

*Panorama of the arrival
at Perrache station,
Lumière Brothers*

obscurity by specializing in obsolete pre-film media such as flick-books.

Nearly 40 years after its premature curtailment, the work of the Skladanowsky Brothers was abruptly resurrected in one of the supreme aberrations of film history. In 1935, the National Socialist government in Germany seized on the then-aged and forgotten Max Skladanowsky, representing him as the pre-eminent world-wide pioneer of film, in order to counter the status of the Lumière Brothers as cinema's primary inventors. An official plaque was unveiled at the Wintergarten to emphasize that it had been in Germany, rather than in France or the US, that the first screening had been held, and the Skladanowsky Brothers' film images of Berlin briefly became a matter of elation and prestige once again. But during the first moments of the Second World War, on 30 November 1939, Max Skladanowsky died in Berlin; by the war's end, the volatile city whose buildings and inhabitants he had filmed for the first time had been virtually obliterated.[1]

By the opening of the twentieth century, the film city had amassed into a vast accumulation of bodies and gestures, of urban surfaces and movements. Across every European country, film-makers caught images of human processions: figures heading into and out of their factories, or following the funeral parades of monarchs and politicians, or entering the alluring pleasure zones of the city. The film image began to play a dominant part in the resolution and placing of human bodies within urban space, their identity defined as that of the inhabitants of a particular city, incorporated within the arena of its buildings and their disparate resonances of poverty or wealth. The great rushes of individual human figures traversed an architectural screen that constantly hovers and flickers in the city's first film images, as though those bodies had become engulfed within the heat of a desert mirage.

The Lumière Brothers' city of Lyons had transformed itself into the paradise of the cinema image by the beginning of the twentieth century: unlike Le Prince's Leeds and the Skladanowsky Brothers' Berlin, films of Lyons showed an Edenic place that was not jarred with momentary intimations of corporeal or urban calamity. In the Lumière Brothers' city films, any sense of an incipient malediction at the heart of cinema's origins dissolved. As the Lumière Brothers collected images of their city across the final years of the nineteenth century, urban space cohered and took on a calm logic, as though it was heading in a determined direction. The magisterial ease with which the Lumière Brothers succeeded in appropriating their status as the innovators of cinema was largely transmitted through their imageries of benign, linear cities – and also through the cosmopolitan fluidity of their travels from capital city to city across Europe, demonstrating their work in highly orchestrated spectacles which only occasionally threatened the audience with an urban conflagration (as happened in London in 1896, during one of the first British film screenings, at the Marlborough Hall of the Polytechnic Institution in Regent Street, where the Lumière Brothers' projector abruptly caught fire).

In the first great tracking-shot of the city – the Lumière Brothers' film *Panorama of the arrival at Perrache station* – the immobile camera passively scans the intricate visual and linguistic textures of the city from a gradually slowing train; with no intention beyond the holding-open of the lens for a duration of 30 seconds as the film passes through the camera, the city's contradictory expanse simply delineates itself. The film appears to have been shot early in the morning: no human figures whatsoever appear. As the train enters the city from the north, the film sequence begins with foreground images of apartment houses running along-side the elevated railway track, while factory chimneys and the outline of the Lyons basilica appear in the nebulous far distance, on a sheer hill. The invisible train passes over a wide river, the mass of shifting currents clearly discernible below a traffic bridge; then, the images show great empty boule-vards flanked by trees. Abruptly, the images become satu-rated with text in the form of three vast advertising screens on the blind side of a tenement block, their veering content declared in fragments of black letters far larger than human forms, and too immediately close to the camera to be read in their entirety. The texts of the city exclaim its essential components as the train enters its mercantile heart: 'grande maison . . . lingerie . . . chapellerie'. The camera finally pans slightly backwards towards the hill over the city as the train decelerates into the Perrache station, its platforms devoid of all corporeal life.

In the city images from cinema's first decade, the pres-ence of the human figure imparts both banality and potential eruption to the medium; the body becomes rapidly positioned by the film image, within its constrictive spaces of work or leisure, but that position remains caustically edged with aber-ration. Even in those first years of the film city – in which its inhabitants pre-eminently stride in tight groups along café-lined boulevards or through factory gates, glaring in astonishment or wilfully oblivious to the camera – the human body forms the image's irrepressible element, always ready to inflict summary reversals on the becalmed city, to generate civil unrest and urban revolution at least in part for the pure elation of its visual depiction and, ultimately, to annul the city itself. At the same time, the camera gradually begins to abandon the passivity with which the first images of film cities had been collected and takes on itself the work of urban invention that would reach its zenith at the end of the 1920s.

During the first years of the twentieth century, the great visual archives of the film city also started to develop, largely through the work of philanthropists who believed that the existence of such image-banks could lead to globalized harmony and understanding, and serve to avert catastrophe. The most exceptional of those visually obsessed philanthropists, the French financier Albert Kahn, feared that the world's cities had already begun to disintegrate and vanish, and urgently needed to be coalesced via the medium of film images; from 1909 on, he assembled a huge team of professional cinematographers and dispatched them to cities across 48 countries, instructing them to bring back an 'archive of the planet'. For two decades – including the span of the First World War – the many thousands of resulting celluloid reels steadily accumulated at Kahn's estate, at Boulogne on the edge of Paris, forming an immense archive of world-wide urban surfaces and human figures. With the onset of the international financial crash of 1929, the bankrupt Kahn's project came to a sudden end, at the very moment of the most intensive experimentation into the forms of the film city.

The city sensationally usurped the medium of cinema in Europe during the final years of the 1920s, when film began to confront the imminence of vocal sonorization and its implications for the autonomy of the image. In every film of the city up until that moment, in the absence of synchronized sound, the image had retained its hallucinatory texture: cities seized the eyes and senses of their spectators in the form of phantom apparitions, as fabulous mirages or as raw incitements to social revolt. Human bodies had been umbilically linked to those images of urban upheaval, the mute figures vividly gesturing across the city's face in elation or negation. But the arrival of synchronized-sound cinema implied the destitution of that evocatory power of the film image as all of the great European experimental film-makers of the period foresaw: vocal sound would trivialize cinema into dramatic narrative forms and open it up to forced global appropriation by Hollywood. While the film image existed in vital flux and constantly induced vertiginous innovation, sound carried with it all of the deadening stasis of spoken language that would fix cinema for the next decade as a subsidiary variant of theatre. As a last stand before the arrival of sound synchronization, a rush of city films appeared across Europe, especially in Germany, France and the Soviet Union, in which the visual city's fluid forms determinedly took pre-eminence, their compelling images engrained with their own imminent vulnerability to archaism. Alongside this ascendant preoccupation with urban space in the final city films of silent cinema, explorations into the intricate forms of the human body plummeted and dissolved; the First World War – disseminated in cinema spaces via newsreels – had spread so many images of mud-encrusted figures locked in intractable combat, and arbitrarily slaughtered in their millions, that corporeal form itself had become irreparably devalorized. As a result, the inhabitants of the film cities of the 1920s possessed a tenuous emotional status, defined only by their basic desires of lust and greed. The perceiving eye supplanted the body, and the matter of vision in the city – with all of its provocative transmutations – formed the essential matter of those 1920s city films.

Walter Ruttmann's *Berlin: The Symphony of the Great City* (1927) opens with a journey by train into the city – an arrival that accelerates rather than slows, accumulating and manipulating a relentless sensory exhilaration, in an inverse strategy to the Lumière Brothers' artless arrival in the seemingly depopulated city of Lyons 30 years earlier. That seminal arrival into the core of the city was replicated in innumerable city films of subsequent years. Once immersed within Berlin, the film (which Ruttmann edited from footage shot in the streets over a period of a year by concealed cinematographers) oscillates between scanning its surfaces, as the ephemeral traces of a day and night pass over its buildings and avenues, and examining the nature of perception in the city, with the camera following the inhabitants' gaze at its incessant spectacle. The inhabitants of Berlin themselves play no part in the city's vital insurgencies and convulsions, which are all generated within the visual matter of the place itself: Ruttmann shows them stampeding into their factories and offices, the images intercut with footage of cattle herded passively through the gates of an abattoir; after dark, those moribund inhabitants pursue a similar regime of self-immolation, via alcohol and lust, in sex cabarets and bars. Only the city itself possesses any dignity and resilience, which it intermittently allows its inhabitants the luxury to perceive through the medium of its illuminations: its neon screens, advertising hoardings and captivating visual displays.

As the title of Ruttmann's film intimates, the city is incorporated within images that are themselves indicative of sonic sweeps and plunges – but that ultimately remain silent, only becoming aurally revivified in screening events through the medium of the multiple sound-tracks attachable to those images. The city films of the late 1920s both caustically refute sound and also invite sonic experiment, since they issue from an era in which the imposition of sound on the image, especially vocal sound, was often viewed with acute unease by directors. The city film-makers usually provided orchestrated scores (Ruttmann himself collaborated on a score for *Berlin: The Symphony of the Great City* with the composer Edmund Meisel, although the original has been lost) or, at least, some fragmentary indications for the desired sonic accompaniment to the projection of their films – only a small scattering of films from the silent era, with very particular perceptual demands on their spectators, were ever actually projected in absolute silence. But in subsequent decades, these city films would induce a need among musicians to amend the existing sound-tracks by creating contemporary sound structures able to deny their own power while enabling the city images to have a more direct impact on the watching eye.

Four years on from Ruttmann's film, on the other side of the arrival of synchronized sound, the space of Berlin dissipated its sense of determined movement, showing its vulnerability to upheaval far more acutely. In Piel Jutzi's 1931 film taken from Alfred Döblin's novel *Berlin Alexander-platz*, the emergent, still-malfunctioning technology of vocal-sound recording sends spoken words reeling, from moment to moment, between cogent audibility and barely registered sonic traces. As if to compensate for the techno-logical frailty of vocal synchronization, the mouth of the actor Heinrich George – playing the character of Franz Biberkopf – blurts cacophonic exclamations, narrating his own release from Tegel prison and subsequent misadven-tures in the form of deliriously asserted monologues. During these years, Berlin's inhabitants perceived the immensely popular George as incorporating and personifying Berlin. At crucial points in the film's narrative – at which the character has been totally shattered and needs to publicly manifest his resilience – Biberkopf stands his ground within the central space of Berlin and directly imposes his presence on the city, through linear streams of vocal self-consolidation. Ostensi-bly promoting the sale of novelty items to the crowds which

Berlin Alexanderplatz, Piel Jutzi

gather around him, he tightly binds together his sonic identity with his corporeal and urban identities, through the
tangible medium of the voice. Around its axis in the figure of
Biberkopf, the space of the Alexanderplatz fractures through
the film's disjointed editing, as sequences chart the area's
intricate visual detail and its human acts in shots of fluctuating length and from variable distances, some synchronized
with the city's sounds, others silent. The images of the

Alexanderplatz (which was undergoing major reconstruction work at the time of the film-shoot) veer sharply from one perspective to another, revealing the vital flaws and gaps in the matter of the city, cohering only through the corporeal presence of Biberkopf's monologues. With sound-recording technology still in a formative state, the city and its sound-track fail to assimilate within *Berlin Alexanderplatz*, thereby enabling the distinctive voice of Biberkopf to conjure up and impose its own off-centre visions.

In *Berlin Alexanderplatz*, the multiple surfaces and layers of the ineptly sonorized city remain uniquely exposed. Over the next few years, advances in sound technology would rapidly bring the film city and its inhabitants together within prosaic narrative forms driven by exchanges of dialogue. Jutzi's film carries the strange moment of technological openness at which vocal sound could work to propel itself across the face of the city, in wayward sonic gestures and ricochets, accentuating the film images' momentary seizure of the transforming urban space. In those images, construction workers abruptly swallow the contents of beer bottles; the architectural surfaces of the Alexanderplatz deliquesce in a midday heat haze; trams precariously cross hollowed-out space on tracks poised above excavations; children ride tricycles through the dense physical crush; and advertising texts project themselves, inscribed with infinite repetition across the façades of buildings, on human billboards and over the side-panels of buses and trams. The city is visually assembled as a constellation of volatile gestures, each with its rapidly superseded hold on time. Behind all of those collective, isolated acts, Biberkopf's ever-present and omniscient voice narrates his individual calamities. Ahead of those human inhabitants immersed in the pulsating centre of the city, a decade or so on, there lay the cancellation of all of their urban surfaces and sounds, with the wholesale extinguishing of the Alexanderplatz by war-time bombing. Even Heinrich George, the unstoppable voice of Berlin, would be silenced: accused of complicity with the National Socialist regime and incarcerated after the fall of Berlin by the occupying Soviet forces, he died of ill treatment in September 1946 at the former concentration camp of Sachsenhausen, on the edge of Berlin.

The great preoccupation with the matter of the city in European experimental cinema of the late 1920s engendered some of the most aberrant images of urban space in the history of film. Extending beyond the form of those documentary projects which portrayed particular cities as determining the acts, gestures and perception of their inhabitants, the concern with the city's power permeated even the most internally inflected films of that moment. The visualization of an obsession with the process of dreaming or with sexual compulsions, as in the films of the Surrealists, occurred within the city's impacting space. In Germaine Dulac's *The Seashell and the Clergyman*, shot in Paris in 1927 and based on a scenario by the legendary theorist Antonin Artaud (who had originally intended to direct the film himself), a narrative of internalized preoccupations – with seminal fluids, violent sexual degradation and human enslavement – abruptly bursts out into images of the streets of Paris, where the film's characters relentlessly pursue one another through deserted, sunlit avenues. The exploration of multiple or hallucinated states of consciousness becomes refracted through its insistence on images of the city – images that are themselves layered on one another, in the form of superimposed and variably reiterated sequences – that serve to situate the film's capricious characters within the substance of their urban surroundings.

One of the few films of the period conceived explicitly to be projected in absolute silence – Artaud detested the emergent sound cinema and had intended this film to wield a mesmeric, purely visual influence on its audience – *The Seashell and the Clergyman* was suddenly transformed at the moment that it entered the hostile arena of the city: its première at the Ursulines cinema on 9 February 1928. There, it was screened to an audience including its director and scenarist, together with a number of unruly Surrealists intent on provoking a disruption of the event. A number of varying accounts of the screening exist.[2] Neither Dulac nor Artaud belonged to the Surrealist movement at that time (Artaud had already been expelled, and Dulac had never joined), but Artaud had protested to Dulac at being excluded from contributing to the direction of the film, and the Surrealists had arbitrarily decided to support him in his quarrel. The film was denounced as being contrary to their own conception of cinema's future. Shortly after the screening began, a fierce riot broke out in the

The Seashell and the Clergyman, Germaine Dulac

cinema stalls, with the Surrealists pelting the screen with debris as images passed over it, fighting with other members of the audience and yelling insults at the director. The projection was abandoned in disarray as Artaud and the Surrealists ran out into the rue des Ursulines, screaming and yelling, and using their fists to shatter the glass panels in the cinema's foyer. All planned projections of the film were cancelled, and it disappeared into the far peripheries of cinema history.

The city exerts an overwhelmingly subjugating force around the corporeal presences in Dulac's film. The figure dressed as a priest is seen shuffling along on his knees in fear through the streets and alleyways of Montmartre. Intercut with his gestures, shaking images shot from the front of a slowly advancing vehicle seize the streets as a void imposition on human life. The buildings on either side of the avenues duplicate themselves as the camera passes between them, so that the city loses its definitive quality and dissolves into juxtaposed screens of urban movement. (Dulac, one of the very few women directors working in France during that period, proved to be expert in utilizing technological innovations for the combining and superimposition of film images.) After experiencing a shock of sexual jealousy, the priest rises from his knees in fury and begins to run through the streets, holding his arms stiffly alongside his body; the sequences replicate themselves as he turns corner after corner in pursuit of the two figures who have incited his anger. The self-absorbed priest is seen to catch the attention of the city's other inhabitants at only one point: as he runs in front of the reflecting plate glass of a large shop window, a number of bemused Parisians appear, standing in a line, awestruck at his bizarre behaviour, and the film jolts momentarily from its own interior preoccupations to fix a documentary detail of the city. Dulac's Surrealist world becomes abruptly entangled with that of Paris's street life, captured by chance on a sunlit summer day in 1927.

The Seashell and the Clergyman served to initiate the

strategy in city films by which an internal world is abruptly shattered through the passage of a character into the conflictual exterior space of the street. Such a transition carries the violence that the summary cancellation of an obsession or dream entails, imparting the volatile emotional charge of the character's preoccupations to the space of the city itself. The director Luís Buñuel, who attended the première of Dulac's film, used the same strategy of showing deviant movements between internal and urban landscapes in what became the authoritative film of the Surrealist movement, *Un Chien Andalou*, made in collaboration with Salvador Dalí (Buñuel attended the première of his own film with his pockets full of stones, mistakenly fearing that it would provoke the same kind of furore as had *The Seashell and the Clergyman*). And European film cities of the decades after the Second World War would again become illuminated by such transmutations of vision, as their characters crossed between the contradictory worlds of the city and of human obsession. But the onset of cinema with synchronized sound cast Buñuel's film into a temporary oblivion during the 1930s, alongside Dulac's work; the moment at which film could explore the wildly fluctuating matter of the city, through the medium of exigent visual experimentation, appeared then to its proponents to have evanesced forever.

At the end of the 1920s, the films associated with (or assaulted by) the Surrealist movement were shown in small cinemas in Paris that were dedicated to screening innovative work – the Ursulines in Montparnasse and the Studio 28 in

Montmartre, where Artaud would make a final, desperate plea for the total separation of the film image from sound, in a lecture delivered in June 1929. These films existed, for that moment, outside the domain of the cinema culture of the Parisian boulevards, where the dialogue-encrusted melodramas which Artaud denounced soon came to saturate the screens of the city's lavish film-palaces, with their multi-tiered auditoriums and vast audiences, alongside Hollywood films. Those sound films, with their accompanying stars, instituted a form of French cinema that came to be viewed as incorporating national character or aspirations – often caustically so, as in the glowering 1930s films of Marcel Carné, set in the marginal tenement districts of Paris – at a time when France was set to propel itself into national freefall, its colonial power increasingly unravelling while European fascism consolidated itself. But even after the coming of sound, the Ursulines and Studio 28 cinemas survived (as they have up to the present moment), pragmatically switching their function to that of cinemas frequented by the inhabitants of the calm surrounding streets, but still infused by the abrasive traces of the great riots and manifestoes of experimental film.

The exploration of the rapport between perception and the city took place at its maximum intensity in the pre-eminent city film of the late 1920s, Dziga Vertov's *The Man with the Movie Camera*, shot in a number of cities of the Soviet Union in 1928, during the same period as the riot surrounding Dulac's *The Seashell and the Clergyman* in Paris. And, while

*The Man with the Movie
Camera*, Dziga Vertov

explicitly a documentary on the forms of the city, Vertov's
film is in many ways more allied with Dulac's than with linear
urban works such as *Berlin: The Symphony of the Great City*:
Vertov's urban focus propels the city at speed into a vast
delirium of images, in infinite flux and often independent of
one another, so that the spectator is compelled to re-create
the film at every viewing (as with Dulac's film), with divergent

outcomes each time. Vertov's inciting of and challenge to the spectator's perception results in the salutary accumulation of contradictory variants of the city: it is unfixed, unhinged, torn open to transformation. But his film possesses its own sense of uniqueness, albeit one that is negatively charged: poised at the moment before the synchronization of dialogue (which proved to be as calamitous for a Soviet film-maker like Vertov as it did for experimental cinema in Western Europe),

The Man with the Movie Camera simultaneously resists the oncoming precipice of Stalinist film culture.

Vertov conceived his film literally as a manifesto on the exhilarating power which cinema could exert on the city and its spectators. In the textual declarations which open his film, Vertov particularly rejects the amalgamation of film with theatre and acting; separating out his own inflammatory project for cinema from all other visual media, he announces it as an 'international' experiment (for which he situates himself as the 'author-supervisor'), with the potential to explode the growing homogeneity and banalization that was permeating cinema at that time. The emphasis on an internationality in Vertov's vision of the city serves to fire his work with the initial revolutionary impetus of the Soviet Union, which had entirely dissipated from its political and social dimensions by that moment. Although *The Man with the Movie Camera* would join most other city films in having multiple sound-tracks unwillingly attached to its images in the decades after its making, in 1996 the silent-film historian Paolo Cherchi Usai and his colleagues successfully reconstructed Vertov's original indications for the sound-track. The resulting film – rendered instantly archaic on its completion in 1929 – now forms the most vitally contemporary document of the human eye in the city.

Vertov begins his film at dawn, with an awakening of the eye: the iris of the camera and the lens of the projector, and also the startled ocular movements of the destitute inhabitants of Odessa, sleeping on benches or by the roadside, their first vision of the day being Vertov's cameraman scanning their waking faces and fitful gestures. The inhabitants of the city react with humour or anger to this intrusion, which continues relentlessly throughout the film, tracking the intimate details of interlocking urban and physical surfaces. Through super-imposition, the film camera is placed high above the city, its totalitarian visual power ironically idolized, but also prescient of the exhaustive systems of mass surveillance that would accompany the Stalinist purges and post-war Eastern European regimes. Where Ruttmann's film charts the ephemeral passage of a day and night over Berlin, Vertov too starts filming at dawn, but then fractures the city's entire temporal structure, pursuing his own obsessions and juxtapositions among its multiply shifting elements. The film city is assembled via random compulsions and determined insights. The city's discreet identity is itself eroded, since Vertov compacts disparate urban space from a number of far-flung Soviet cities, from Moscow to Odessa, in order to create a composite, disunified place able to refract his experiments on perception. Although Vertov gives priority to images of factories and drinking halls, and to human gestures of work and pleasure, above all he probes the capacity of the eye to generate and receive, at speed, the raw essence of revolutionary images.

Vertov splits his film images of the city and its buildings apart, with a vertical division along the centre of the frame, and then pivots the two halves together, so that the city suddenly pours into itself with a visual rush. Where Dulac multiplied the city through superimposition, Vertov disassembles its substance into components for reactivated urban forms. Under the impact of rapid editing, the city appears and disappears with such volatility that the work required of the spectator's eye itself constitutes a new component of vision. At one point, the car carrying Vertov's cameraman veers so quickly through the streets that a human figure can be seen leaping out of the way in order literally to avoid death by film-speed.

The cinema itself forms a crucial axis in Vertov's project: the motivation for the film emerges from the empty cinema shown at the beginning which then fills to capacity for the screening towards its end. The city's inhabitants, packed together on their wooden seats in the darkness, trans-fixed in anticipation, require a collective visual event in order for the film to become a corporeally and memorially resonant experience. The cinema – its architecture and its rituals of human entrance and exiting – gathers a revelatory presence for itself within the space of the city. In the course of his work on the 'film-trains' which toured the vast expanse of the Soviet Union at the beginning of the 1920s, Vertov had shot, edited and projected films in the space of a few hours, so that the inhabitants of isolated rural communities who had rarely seen films before would recognize their own images – usually engaged in gruelling manual labour – on the walls of impromptu cinema spaces. But in *The Man with the Movie Camera*, it is the city itself which is minutely disassembled, reconstructed and revivified, and finally projected back to itself.

In every European country, the arrival of synchronized cinema and the pre-eminence of theatrically derived film dialogue curtailed the work of those film-makers who had intensively probed the visual, sensory and sonic emanations of the city at the end of the 1920s: film-makers as diverse as Ruttmann, Vertov and Buñuel all found their work consigned to oblivion during the 1930s. In the Soviet Union, the coming of sound cinema coincided with the consolidation of Stalin's power. While Vertov's career ran definitively into the lost margins of Soviet cinema, the other great director of the experimental film-train projects, Alexander Medvedkin, was able to accommodate himself to some degree with the transformed film culture, and it was he who captured the most revealing images of Stalin's Moscow. A committed Communist, Medvedkin's work on the film-trains had been intricately riven with contradictions: while exhorting the inhabitants of the Stalinist pioneer cities to work ceaselessly in producing the materials for the construction of new cities, he had also filmed images of the bureaucracy which impeded such constructions, the factory workers disgraced as saboteurs for execution, and the conditions that brought about the mass famines on the Ukrainian collective farms, where millions died of starvation and disease. Medvedkin's engaged participation in the social upheavals around the end of the 1920s – when the potential of cinema could still infuse film-makers with a revolutionary passion – generated an element of dissidence in his approach to the more linear depiction of the Soviet Union's urban forms in the subsequent decade.

New Moscow, Alexander
Medvedkin

Even in his work within the heart of Stalin's film industry, Medvedkin created irrepressibly deviant images of the Soviet Union's new urban aspirations. Stalin himself formulated plans for the reconstruction of Moscow; like Hitler and Speer with their vast models for the redesigning of Berlin, Stalin's architectural ambitions for his capital extended deliriously into an idealized future in which colossal edifices surmounted by statues of Soviet leaders would line the city's avenues. In Medvedkin's *New Moscow* (1938), that projected city is seen to go haywire, and its past, present and future are incorporated in one hallucinatory misfiring. The key sequence takes place at a prestigious cinema screening where the city's architects are presenting a film of their plans. But the projector malfunctions, so that the images jam abruptly, layering on one another in the form of superimpositions, and then reverse in time, so that Stalin's ambitions are negated, and Moscow's archaic forms – its grand cathedrals and Tsarist buildings – become presciently resuscitated as the aberrant, contemporary Moscow. And when the malfunctioning projection of the city is corrected, and the celluloid begins to run smoothly forward through linear time, the forms of the new city appear even more untenable than before, surreal and insanely grandiose.

Medvedkin's *New Moscow* offended the Soviet censors (Stalin personally watched and judged every film made in his domain) and immediately disappeared from view; Stalin's great plans for Moscow, like those of Hitler and Speer, remained largely unrealized. Instead, the immovable form of Stalin himself gradually came to embody and becalm the city whose heated visual transmutations Vertov, above all, had provoked; in the second half of the 1930s, Stalin's figure appeared in many fiction films, played by a glowering actor whose pensive features replaced the dictator's own aging, pockmarked face in the perception of Soviet citizens. His corporeal interventions in the city served especially to reassure its population on matters of technological

New Moscow, Alexander
Medvedkin

or mechanical mishap: in one film, he appears in Red Square at the moment when a passing tractor has broken down there, to the dismay of the gathered inhabitants; omnisciently diagnosing the problem, he mends the tractor and then serenely rides out of the frame at its wheel. That filmic embodiment by Stalin of Moscow would reach its fulfilment when the invading German army almost reached the city in the autumn of 1941, and Stalin's obdurate figure appeared in (faked) film footage, disseminated in newsreel screenings to the city's panic-stricken inhabitants, to prove that he had not fled and would remain in the city, whose population then also resolved to hold out.

Medvedkin's own total submission to the visual imperatives of Stalin's Moscow came with his film of the 1939 Mayday parade, *Blossoming Youth*. No irony or dissidence remains in the images of the endless celebratory parade and of the portraits of Stalin and his acolytes emblazoned over the city's façades. This film serves to seamlessly establish the rapport between Stalin on his podium and Moscow's youthful inhabitants, fixed in physical displays of elation as they pass by and momentarily oblivious to the oncoming European conflict that would decimate millions of the Soviet Union's young population and leave many of its cities in ruins. Medvedkin's final images of the pre-war city and its young figures suspend that rigorously choreographed moment of time under Stalin's gaze, infinite worlds away from the revolutionary urban uproar and speed of Vertov's images from a decade earlier.

Europe's film cities existed largely through the medium of newsreel during the subsequent years of conflict. With the exception of Humphrey Jennings's wartime experiments in recreating the perception of Britain by means of short films that allied intricate elements of fiction or invention with surreal strategies of documentary, fiction films across Europe largely became confined to cramped interior melodrama and exhortative propaganda. Cinema spectators

Film image of Berlin at the end
of the Second World War

were mesmerized by spectacular newsreel images of the
burning streets of London or Hamburg and by snatched
frames of combatants struggling their way through the gradually more devastated urban terrain of Europe. The sky
directly above cities took on an unprecedented importance as
their inhabitants and film-makers minutely scanned it for the
sonic and visual traces of arriving bombers. The subterranea
of cities in meltdown expanded as their populations escaped
the lethal ground level. Entire cities suddenly emptied out,
their inhabitants expelled or carbonized. For the first time,
the film image held cities that were visually defined by genocide and depopulation.

The film images of the destroyed cities of Europe, recorded
from aeroplanes flying above them in April and May 1945,
form one of the punctuation points in the depiction by film
of urban space. All of the waves of social and political

contestation which had convulsed those cities, and the entirety of Europe, from the period of Louis Le Prince's first film of the industrial façades of Leeds vanished now in those images of eviscerated tenements, blasted palaces and mixed human and architectural ashes. The decades from the end of the nineteenth century to the mid-point of the twentieth had been visually scored by two interlocked urban cultures: film culture, which had captivated the senses of Europe's population and had strewn the central boulevards of its capitals with luxurious cinemas, and social culture, which had participated in the industrial and commercial transmutations of urban life, in the complicities and confrontations between fascist and Communist regimes – marked out in city space by parades and street battles – and, in 1945, in the summary disappearance of human figures from the face of many European cities. The newsreel images of urban Europe in its devastation constituted an enduring zero interval in the history of the city.

Most of the newsreel images of destroyed European urban landscapes focused on German cities: the buildings emptied out, often reduced to a scattering of jagged debris at the edges of barely recognizable avenues. During the final weeks of the war, such aerial images had been shot as potential indicators of the moment when an exhausted Germany might be predicted to capitulate; in earlier months, films taken from night-bombing raids over phosphorescent cities had similarly served to predict which un-hit urban or industrial areas should next be targeted. But once the war had finished, those newsreel images (almost always framed as slow, linear tracking shots) were rendered explicitly as images of victory: projected world-wide, they demonstrated that the conception of victory could be seized by spectators primarily or even solely through the visual cancellation of enemy cities. The post-war history of Europe began with a sense of elation at such annulments, and cinema advanced its importance as a medium by signalling the ways in which film images (rather than those of other visual media such as photography or painting) possessed the capacity, via their powerful ocular movement and emotional resonances, to determine the perception of urban forms.

Beyond Europe, too, film scanned urban landscapes in parallel states of incineration; in Tokyo, cameras filming from the ground – their operators in severe danger – caught the illuminated trajectories of the bombs that descended on the city, precipitating the same kind of firestorms which had already been filmed in Dresden and Hamburg. A unique film language of the devastated city locked together the cities of Europe and Japan at that moment, from Berlin and London to Hiroshima and Tokyo, and shaped the ways in which cinema would approach urban forms internationally in the decades after the war. The film city and its inhabitants now began to emanate an aura of precarious insubstantiality – their forms infinitely subject to amendment or even cancellation – that had been completely absent both from the exhilarated urban images of Vertov and the more solid fiction-film images of directors such as Piel Jutzi. The ultimate realization of that movement towards urban and corporeal disappearance would only come with the onset of the digital image five or six decades later. But the images of international urban ruination in 1945 mark a moment of fracture from which the film city began to collapse upon itself.

In Europe, the film images of the human body which pre-eminently accompanied these urban images were those of the executed Mussolini, hung upside-down in the Piazzale Loreto in Milan, and of a corpse then mistakenly assumed to be that of Hitler, in the grounds of the Chancellery in Berlin; those dead figures were set against the triumphant ones, poised on balconies, of Churchill in London and Stalin in Moscow, receiving the acclamation of immense crowds. On a more anonymous level, the end of the war sent great columns of refugees across the blackened surfaces of Europe. Many fiction films of the next few years – such as those made in the emergent East German state, occupied by the Soviet army – would track the individual journeys made by members of such lost populations, through hazardous interstitial landscapes, back to their often unrecognizable cities; even journeys within the space of the ruined city, such as those undertaken in Roberto Rossellini's *Germany Year Zero* (1947), filmed in Berlin's scrambled terrain, form perilous human transits between effaced points of departure and arrival. In newsreel images, the return of millions of now-redundant soldiers from war zones to cities formed a key visual preoccupation. A fundamental mismatch between the damaged corporeal and architectural elements of the city emerged: on their return, the displaced bodies and voices of the city could no longer cohere with its surfaces and façades in ways that had been possible before the conflict. The sense of a European 'home' had been shattered. Concurrently, in films dealing with urban life, the forms that seemed to have been permanently set in the pre-war years now appeared far more fragile: in particular, the seamless synchronization between image and sound that had marked both fiction and documentary cinema of the 1930s would soon show signs of breaking down. European urban space started to evolve a new set of transformations.

The origins of the film city were carried within a momentum of exploration and calamity. Originally advanced by the technological or spectacular preoccupations of figures such as Louis Le Prince and the Skladanowsky Brothers, the film city soon gathered a dimension of power for itself. All of the political transmutations that marked out the first half of the twentieth century – the great urban battles between fascist and Communist systems, the ascendancies of corporate culture within the city – became embedded and refracted within the film image; similarly, the power to debase or elevate human forms and acts mediated itself through cinema. Film images developed the authority to accord validity or veracity to such acts and physical gestures, or to withdraw it; they could also create borders around and within the space of the city, visualizing the expulsion of human elements foreign to it and containing those elements which became viewed as its rightful inhabitants. (Stigmatized elements of a population could also be rigidly contained within the space of the city via the film image, as in the films of the Warsaw Ghetto.) At moments of historical crisis, such as that of 1945, film exercised its capacity to combine many seemingly contrary materials; eventually, the unique contribution of the digital image to this strategy would be to enable those few materials which film had never managed to combine, such as nostalgia and atrocity, to be compacted within the span of one image. The space of the city formed the primary site within which visual media collided and amalgamated with one another, across space and time, from the very origins of film. For all its infinite enchantments and attractions, the city formed a ferocious zone of conflict for cinematic imagery.

2 urban space in european cinema

Film images of European cities illuminate the past and future of urban forms; the crises and sensations of city inhabitants are projected through European cinema's infinite capacity to juxtapose urban and corporeal identity within a contrary rapport which may be coruscating or cohering, according to each director's particular set of human and technological caprices and convictions. The images that emerge from that raw zone of contact between the human figure and the city provide intricately revealing indicators of Europe's contemporary moment.

In the decades after the Second World War, a primary preoccupation of European cinema was the slow-burning impact on cities and their inhabitants of that conflict's residue. While the Cold War rapidly developed its own momentum within the political and media cultures of Europe, resuscitating their often exhausted or moribund institutions, the architectural forms of its cities recoiled from the conflict in another way. Immense building programmes, often executed at high speed, replaced destroyed or damaged districts, configuring a pattern of endless concrete tenements that grew over the subsequent decades, proliferating across Europe's impoverished cities and forming the location for much of the vital urban film-making of that period. Long-standing inner-city communities were dispersed into suburban areas, and the dominant human and architectural fixation of European cinema became that of displacement. The unremitting journey of work from the peripheral suburbs to the city centre inspired a visual banality that jarred with all of those unique and elated entries into urban space from the city films of the late 1920s.

European cinema increasingly explored an obsession with exile that had originated in part with the lost trajectories of mass refugee populations in the post-war years; innumerable styles and technologies of exile grew to suffuse and support that filmic obsession. Exile articulated itself in contradictory forms: in the urban context, the city's inhabitants habitually found themselves positioned within abrasive or unrecognizable environments; exile articulated itself directly, in the form of a corporeal system under intense strain, its fractures and sensory implosions pre-eminently mediated through the eyes. The filmic depiction of exile in the city encompassed that of its transitory or nomadic inhabitants, caught momentarily within the hostile and expulsive system of a particular place, and also that of citizens who had never been displaced, but had instead perceived the comprehensive upheaval of the city around them, which erased from itself all of their focal points of stability. The film city of exile, together with its suburbs, irrepressibly transmuted and cancelled its forms, while inflicting seismic transformation on the bodies and visual perception of its inhabitants.

European film-makers often became preoccupied in those post-war decades with the idea of urban space being integrally decayed and ruined, the cities enveloped by mysteriously corroded wastelands. Anxiety over a number of 'lost' Europes developed through the medium of cinema in the 1950s and '60s: in one such form, Europe appeared to have fallen under the grip of a malediction, whose axis lay in its troubled cities; in another form, Europe had certainly once existed (if only in film images), but had now irreparably fractured and vanished, along with its constituent imperial, national and urban identities. Allied to this sense of loss was a preoccupation with memory: Europe could only be revivified if it could be remembered; its cities' inhabitants, too, existed in a state of oblivion of their spiritual or physical capacities. Activating the memory of Europe constituted a vital matter. But memory – never tractable – could only ever emerge at unexpected, unplanned moments in the European film image, often in its most inept or ludicrous forms.

Heading towards the contemporary moment, that unease in European cinema turned to the idea of urban space as being increasingly in flux, with the continent's visual cultures subject to 'exterior' images, notably from the US, Japan and North Africa; those images could exert a salutary creative regeneration, but could also intrusively supplant the distinctive visual forms of Europe (just as Europe, in its turn, had in the past often supplanted other cultures). Finally, with the onset of the digital image and its corporate contexts, European film-makers became preoccupied with the erosion of their status both as 'European' and as 'film-makers'; aberrant or independent visual cultures abruptly appeared more homogenous, exposed to arbitrary concentrations of power wielded by multinational media conglomerates. Both the European film image and its densely inscribed urban space now seemed endangered.

The fractured urban space of Europe's post-war years, traversed by forces of historical upheaval, is most revealingly probed in a fiction film produced by a Hollywood studio, Jacques Tourneur's *Berlin Express*, made in 1948 by the RKO studio and featuring such stars as Robert Ryan and Merle Oberon. In *Berlin Express*, the mystery-film genre is used to activate an exploration of the ruined and displaced forms of Europe's cities. Like the early work of Vertov and Medvedkin, *Berlin Express* is explicitly a train film – but with an almost contrary approach to that of the Soviet directors' exhortative experiments: the film's oblivious characters travel through decimated urban landscapes, occasionally disembarking into the vanished avenues of Frankfurt and Berlin as they acrimoniously conspire and struggle among themselves. The film's linear narrative is stranded in lost time, at the moment when German reunification still appeared feasible and desirable from an American perspective. Its plot centres on the need to ensure that a key political figure in the reunification plans reaches an important conference in Berlin, while attempts to kidnap and assassinate him are pursued by fascist saboteurs (the so-called 'werewolves', driven by nostalgia for Hitler's genocides) operating within the humiliated Germany, its area provisionally carved up between its four occupying powers. A small group of American, Soviet and other European figures, in transit through Germany's wasteland, reluctantly bands together to rescue the politician when he disappears. But in its closing moments, the Hollywood film veers into a denunciation that finally allies it with the exhortative strategies of Medvedkin's train films, as it castigates the Soviet occupiers for their obstinacy in planning what soon proved to be the division of Germany.

Berlin Express refracts the visual textures of the disassembled city. With its technically adept Hollywood crew shooting entirely on location, it generates unique images at stylistic variance from the grainy, shaky footage which habitually recorded that urban zero ground, filmed in haste for newsreels. As the characters wander at night through the moribund city, the ruins are transformed into an extraordinarily beautiful and lush terrain of startling shapes and intense shadows, richly rendered in monochrome contrasts. The film draws out both the aesthetic layers and the historical fractures of the city: its voice-over caustically describes how the almost-untouched remains of once-grandiose buildings (including those designed by Speer and Hitler) have been eroded by wind and rain through three post-war winters into bleak but visually compelling configurations which signal a salutary draining of

Berlin Express, Jacques
Tourneur

fascist Europe's overheated urban ambition. The city has largely turned to dust, its surviving inhabitants invisibly starving among the wreckage and measuring time through the units of black-market cigarettes.

Berlin Express probes the status of the body in the city – both that of the ruins' prostituted, apathetic inhabitants and that of the film's central characters, striding through the avenues of Frankfurt as they undertake their search for the kidnapped politician, and commenting incessantly on their own journey through a city whose very geography has to be reconstructed and re-imagined as they enter what they bitterly deride as 'a world in rubble'. Their only excursion beyond that terrain of invariably levelled landscapes comes in the form of a visit to the intact corporate headquarters of I. G. Farben (one of the German chemical conglomerates most actively involved in organizing slave-labour and death camps), whose vast building is being used by the American military authorities. The obliteration of the German cities is made to appear beneficial, while the rare surviving buildings possess an insidious aura of horror. Towards the end of the film, the characters finally leave their train and part in the centre of Berlin, their corporeal forms poised in heroic isolation against the jagged, burned outlines of the Brandenburg Gate and the Reichstag. The seminal sites of the destroyed city are relegated to becoming a filmic backdrop for the attitudes and declamations of Europe's new figures of power.

For almost its entire length, *Berlin Express* appears as a strange hallucination of Europe in crisis, compacted from chaotic urban debris; the film's characters are perpetually at a loss to know how to proceed, and their narrative actions are given momentum only by the most coincidental or gratuitous occurrences. The opaque plot appears to have been largely improvised on the spot. But in its movement through chaos, the film seizes twentieth-century Europe at its most vulnerable interval. It coheres only in its final moments, when its principal American character confronts his Soviet counterpart with the statement that only international understanding will lead to any kind of resolution for the shattered forms of Europe. The Soviet character, initially resistant, eventually capitulates to the American's position, seemingly receptive to future dialogue that may lead to the reunification of Germany. Outside the world of the film, time would move on into the intensification of the Cold War – itself an obsession whipped into prominence by Hollywood cinema – and the long-term division of Germany. The historical aspirations voiced in *Berlin Express* almost immediately descended into archaism, while its visual grip on the ruined panoramas of Europe (similar in their expansiveness to the Skladanowsky Brothers' Nebula spectacles of 60 years earlier) became ever more vital as the redundant film advanced into the future.

In 1991, the year following the eventual reunification of Germany, the Danish director Lars von Trier made his sombre film *Europa*, which in many ways forms a kind of remake, in negative, of *Berlin Express*. Again, the film's action takes place pre-eminently on a dark, hurtling train, on which an earnest young American of European descent is attempting to contribute to the reconstruction of post-war Germany by working as a steward. But the damaged urban landscapes around him prove so disorienting that he finds himself lost, increasingly overwhelmed by the contrary vocal demands of the various groups he encounters – tainted industrialists, American soldiers and seductive 'werewolves' intent on sabotage. Driven into a frenzy, he finally blows up his own train, which plummets from a bridge into a river, with him still trapped in one of the carriages. The final underwater images show the diminishing gestures of the drowning man trying desperately to free himself. Von Trier's character appears omnisciently conscious both of the ravaged post-war Europe in which the film is set and of the human dilemmas and media delirium of contemporary Europe in the wake of its transformations in 1989. In *Europa*, those two time zones interlock and flow into one another. Contemporary Europe becomes a suffocating experience, its cities remaining unsalvageable, perpetually engrained with a desire for ruination which propels their displaced inhabitants into mental freefall.

In the same year that *Berlin Express* conjured its images of an aesthetically destroyed city from the pounded-down dust of Berlin, the Italian director Vittorio de Sica made the pre-eminent post-war film of the human figure pinioned within the brutal spaces of the city, *Bicycle Thieves*. Although its specific social and political intentions – to delineate a variant of reality in the Rome of the late 1940s – have largely drained away, the film's exploration of the strategic humiliation exerted by the city on its inhabitants remains vivid. The film appeared at the moment of a great resurgence of images of the human figure in European art, particularly in painting and sculpture: in Paris, especially, Jean Dubuffet, Henri Michaux and Alberto Giacometti were all emphasizing raw corporeal matter as the primary creative element in a project of self-willed human resuscitation that often abrasively juxtaposed the city's layered façades with the bodies of its inhabitants.

The cinematic counterpart of this new prominence of the human figure, in films such as *Bicycle Thieves*, produced less volatile but equally evocative results. As in the figurative visual art of that moment, every gesture of urban struggle in de Sica's film is determined by the imminence with which a seminal loss may be exacted on the human body. The arbitrary power of dispossession hangs over every head, provoking responses of resistance or submission.

For a few moments, at the beginning of the film, the acts of the impoverished bicyclist Ricci appear to be exactly attuned with those of the city around him. His work is to cover the city's already-saturated façades with new exclamations of image and text in the form of cinema posters. He meticulously pastes the glowing figure of the Hollywood star Rita Hayworth over the desiccated walls of a miserable street; the vast form of the star's face erupts in sexual splendour, palped by Ricci's hands: the smile is made of flamboyant flesh, the teeth glare brilliantly into the city. The poster adds an extra dimension to the vital concealment of the city's abject surfaces. For that split second, Ricci contributes to the city's life. But at the very next moment, everything is lost, and he abruptly falls into expulsion: a gang of thieves nonchalantly steals his bicycle while he remains magnetized, face to face with Hayworth's adhesive-smeared image.

Throughout the remainder of the film, Ricci's futile search for his bicycle is impeded by the long journey he is repeatedly forced to make between the centre of Rome and his home in the moribund suburbs, where his destitute family

Bicycle Thieves, Vittorio
de Sica

inhabit a cramped flat in one of the innumerable concrete-
block satellites hastily constructed across Europe after the war.
The city's central zone is the only place in which Ricci can
access the means to survive – but, with the theft of his bicycle,
that survival is threatened, so that he remains adrift between
city and suburb, barred from participation in the city's activity
and from returning to the suburb, where no means of existence can be generated among the unvarying blocks. *Bicycle*

Thieves served to initiate a corrosive imagery of suburban space as the site for concentrated human tension – an imagery developed in many disabused city films of subsequent decades. In Mathieu Kassovitz's *La Haine* (1995), for example, the displaced characters' oscillation between the city's expulsive centre and the lethal outskirts works to configure the riot-inflamed suburbs literally as the city's terminal point. Suburban space contradicts that of the city: its alien life is grafted onto the city's resistant body and is connected to it by only the most unworkable of human channels.

In stasis at the city's bus and tram stops, Ricci's body meshes into the infinite queues of figures pressed up against one another. In another film of the congealed city, Chantal Akerman's *D'Est* (1993), which scans the crowds packed around suburban tram stops in the collapsed Soviet Union, the individual gazes of the waiting figures lock together into a mass glare of blank hostility at the film-maker's visible camera. Each commuting journey possesses its own time system, suddenly jarring from stillness to urgent movement, its silent horror mediated through the travellers' vacant eyes. In *Bicycle Thieves*, the bodies seen intimately jostling around the tram stops similarly exist in isolated temporal zones. The hordes of redundant figures stalled in the city serve to mirror the vision of countless bicycles left unguarded outside a football stadium, the sight of which finally provokes Ricci into his own calamitous act of theft.

In the final images of *Bicycle Thieves* – after he has been caught in the act of stealing a bicycle, then released out of pity – Ricci is striding away down the street, poised among the almost identical inhabitants of the city, his figure distinguished only by its utter humiliation (witnessed by his young son), which sends him weeping over the edge of the filmic world. In its examination of the urban denuding of post-war Europe, *Bicycle Thieves* espouses the romance of poverty in order to dispute it, and the baser the level it explores, the greater is the quantity of emotion or outrage it generates. In films of the late 1940s, the monochrome images of Europe's impoverished or ruined cities appear as incitements to act – to invent new cities, to destroy the residue of the old ones still further, to instigate physical or social upheavals. Human figures are shown trapped within suffocating urban environments that work to exact repetition and subjugation. Only film images of the city capture that moment's unique, contrary substance of urban paralysis and insurgence.

By the onset of the 1960s in Europe, the determining visual penury of the post-war period – imprinted deep into its cities' façades and human figures by years of conflict, and then caught within those surfaces and bodies by the film image – had gradually been effaced. The film city still formed a series of excoriating spaces, and the inhabitants crossing that terrain often remained locked within systems of denudation and exploitation. But in the early 1960s, images of the city began to open out into disordered and extravagant forms for the first time since the great city films of the late 1920s. The filmic rendering of the city mutated – in such diverse instances as works by Jean-Luc Godard, Tony Richardson and Dušan Makavejev – its images impelled by capricious strategies of editing into unprecedented configurations which demanded original ocular work from spectators: the city's space collapsed incessantly before the eye, which necessarily reinstated it with variable, multiple emphases. Above all, as the 1960s progressed, the visual city took on sensory inflections from its increasing undercurrents of social dissidence and sexual uproar, which finally burst riotously onto the streets in the decade's final years. The city's habitual arrangement of central corporate districts surrounded by suburban annexes, intended to facilitate financial or political power, was suddenly challenged and even overturned, at least in the resistant imaginations of its inhabitants. The cancellation of those urban forms existed in rapport with the re-sexualized prominence of the human body, generating tensions that were evident both on city streets and in film images. The upheavals of the city could induce active participation, but could also consolidate still further the oblivious stasis of many of its urban and suburban inhabitants. No revolution could ever truly shake the suburbs' integrally moribund form, and in films about the urban zones inhabited by vulnerable figures such as those portrayed by Michelangelo Antonioni, internal corporeal exile often was exacerbated by sexual exploitation or prostitution. The resulting film city of the 1960s is simultaneously one of mutinous urban ecstasy and deep melancholy.

That melancholy of the city is engrained within the opening images of Louis Malle's film *Zazie in the Métro* (1960), where the entry by train into the city (already familiar from innumerable city films, from the Lumière Brothers on) was filmed head-on, so that the camera passed at speed through drained suburban landscapes, heading straight for the city but remaining poised at its edge. Although the film was shot in colour, the urban debris around the railway track appears bleached of any hue; the monotonous vision of distant housing blocks, railway pylons and embankments is

Zazie in the Métro, Louis Malle

Vivre sa Vie, Jean-
Luc Godard

occasionally enlivened by the blur and cacophony of an
express train going in the opposite direction, but the moment
before the city already seems endless. The score accompanying this sequence, by the composer Fiorenzo Carpi, is based
on a repetitively whistled phrase and intimates that the journey could continue indefinitely. The scattered traces of the
oncoming city exude no enticement for the approaching eye,
as they do in such films as *Berlin: The Symphony of the Great*

City. Instead, the eye becomes positioned outside the city, in congealed time, rushing at speed, but inexorably heading nowhere. It takes a jarring ellipsis for that mesmerized eye to finally be heaved into the city and set down within the dense crowds at the Gare de l'Est.

In following the adventures of the ten-year-old Zazie – displaced from the provinces to Paris for a brief interval, before rejoining the train to exit the city once again – the film rapidly disintegrates into evoking human figures in a state of sexual and riotous turmoil, caught within the glare of neon façades. The city's space appears up-ended from its habitual forms, its visual elements deliriously compacted, sonorized by incessant invective as the impudent Zazie berates each of the inhabitants she encounters. No linear narrative can subsist in such a scrambled portrayal – the film shifts from one ludicrous episode to another, taking the form of motiveless chases among gridlocked traffic and of violent insurrections in subterranean drinking spaces. The characters aggressively attempt to seduce one another, in a language of perpetual exclamation, watched over by Zazie's caustic eye. The city's surrounding surfaces are inflected with their own style of exclamation. The film's American designer, William Klein (most notorious for the series of photography catalogues which he was working on at the time, excavating the visual thrall and corporeal gestures of a number of international cities, from New York to Tokyo, in black-and-white panoramas) constructed walls of hoardings imprinted with huge letters, arranged in random, incomprehensible sequences, that reinforce the film's breakdown of urban coherence. In *Zazie in the Métro*, the city's accelerating uproar appears omnipresent; although the inhabitants still speak with nostalgia of events that occurred during the Occupation, Paris now bristles with the volatile visual textures that had begun to mark it at the onset of the 1960s.

However, films that explored the urban layers of Paris in the early 1960s often still seized upon the power of raw degradation exacted by the city, especially in its peripheral areas, rather than its newly instituted sexual furore. The work of the French New Wave directors such as Malle and Godard encompassed a vast, self-contradictory range of preoccupations that negated any idea of their constituting a collective group. In Godard's 1962 monochrome film about Paris and prostitution, *Vivre sa Vie* (It's My Life), the fall and death of the character Nana is depicted against austere urban landscapes – smoky pinball cafés and the views from car windows during journeys through the deserted alleys at the city's edge. Godard divided the sparse material of his narrative into twelve sequences, each one – however banal and inconsequential – contributing its momentum towards the nonchalant instant of his character's murder, as she is maladroitly exchanged between two armed gangs of pimps. The city surrounds each movement – the stylish gestures and dances of the impoverished Nana and the brutal actions of the men controlling her – with its determining aura of fatality; throughout the film, the characters reflect on the nature of free will, but it is clear from the outset that the omniscient director has planned a fatal sacrifice for his 'city-girl'. In Godard's films of the later 1960s, such as *Two or Three Things I Know about Her* (1966), the concrete-block suburbs of Paris served as the focal point for further examinations of prostitution and its imageries; the city's suburbs had proliferated over the previous decade in the form of vast housing blocks overlooking one another, exposing the last nuance of their inhabitants' acts to visual speculation. But in *Vivre sa Vie*, the avenues and alleys of central Paris seep in melancholy around the few brusque gestures that make up the vital material of the film.

During one sequence, Nana escapes from the city's acerbic surfaces in order to hide in a cinema showing Carl Dreyer's silent film *The Passion of Joan of Arc* (1927), with the actress Renée Falconetti as Joan, being prepared for her execution by a monk played by Antonin Artaud. Extracts from Dreyer's film are simply incorporated into Godard's as Falconetti (who would herself end her life working as a prostitute) and Artaud speak about Joan's imminent death: the film is projected in silence, the words articulated by sub-titles. The extract from Dreyer's film is almost entirely composed of intensive close-ups of the wracked faces of Falconetti and Artaud. Occasionally, Godard's film cuts to brief, close-up shots of the face of Nana herself, in the darkness of the empty cinema, transfixed by the film, tears running down her cheeks, as she watches the agonizing images from her own locus of danger. The cinema forms a momentary abyss of darkness, projecting both dread and safety, within the city's over-illuminated face.

Media images of revolution, violence and sex in the cities of
Europe became exceptionally prominent in the late 1960s and
early '70s, accenting every film made during those years.
More than at any moment since the urban destructions of the
Second World War, the form of the city appeared unstable, as
seisms of political dissent, sexual tension and revolutionary
aspiration became situated there, materializing as demonstrations, riots and spectacles. The repression enacted on those
manifestations by governments aimed to stabilize the fracturing city and preserve its corporate structure and power bases.
Throughout those years, in the first vital encounter between
cinema and television media, images of uproar and its violent
suppression saturated the screens of Europe, extending
through every major city in the world, from Santiago to
Tokyo. Political film-makers with disparate, factional preoccupations often grouped together – especially in Paris – in
order to generate alliances among factory workers and exacerbate unrest by castigating the war in Vietnam. A vast,
ephemeral momentum of dissidence began to gather; cinemas
became a primary locus of debate and exhortation, with film
projections often stopped between reel changes for heated
discussion. The city's visual equilibrium was largely thrown
awry by the disruptive film images of that moment, and urban
sensory forms oscillated explosively between political and
corporeal obsessions. But by the early 1970s, with a renewed
consolidation of corporate power in Europe and the dissipation of outcries such as those against the Vietnam War, the
protest movements gradually began to extinguish themselves,

Don't Look Now, Nicolas Roeg

and images of dissidence and sex mutated into ones of loss and death.

The film which most intimately captures that infusion of death into images of the city, Nicolas Roeg's *Don't Look Now* (1973), was shot on location within the disintegrating urban matter of Venice, with two actors who had been deeply involved in the political protests around the end of the previous decade, Donald Sutherland and Julie Christie. Roeg himself had co-directed (with Donald Cammell) *Performance* (1970), a film which tracked the overturning of '60s cultural experimentation into chaotic violence. In the form of a horror mystery, *Don't Look Now* captures the sensation of Europe sliding into dereliction, with Venice as the resonant screen for that descent: the unique visual sensitivity of the city emerges from its having served for many decades as a principal outlet for all of the corruption, illness and lost imperial grandeur of Europe, sluiced into the ocean from its polluted canals. Since the initiatory images of Louis Le Prince, film had always formed a pre-eminent evocatory medium for death in the city. In *Don't Look Now*, haunted, impenetrable Venice articulates a disabused statement of death in the narrative of a couple's journey there to escape the loss of their child. The city immediately surrounds them as a fluctuating space of danger, highlighted by a sound-track of gasps, screams and expirations, every noise magnified by decomposing façades.

In *Don't Look Now*, the city's textures and surfaces hold every element of the narrative, but they must be scrutinized obliquely, and often propelled forwards or backwards in time, in order to become legible. Every indicator of the character John Baxter's imminent murder in Venice is carried either by images on photographs or slides, or in the form of interior images – premonitions, hallucinations and apparitions – or within the mundane visual layers of the city, its alleys and hotel rooms, inscribed on walls, panels and blinds. These elements must be meticulously disassembled in order for Baxter's death to be perceived in its entirety. That event is hidden with the city's flux of time, caught abruptly by flash-forwarded images and, at the moment of his murder at the hands of a serial-killer dwarf whom he has mistaken for the ghost of his dead daughter, by multiple images arranged as flash-backs. The film city strategically disorients its spectators, making them vulnerable to its particular neural shocks: the characters themselves are never entirely certain where they are, or even within which levels of time or consciousness they are living. The opaque, airless city incessantly induces nausea, dizziness, and blackouts. The human figures moving through the canals and alleys remain in perpetual danger – Baxter himself narrowly escapes death several times before his journey into the urban web allows him no further reprieves.

The most notorious sequence of the film is a sex scene in which an anonymous room, in a deserted hotel, in an emptied city, contains the charged, absolute gestures of Baxter and his wife making love (the sequence became renowned at the time for its verisimilitude and its intimation of not being counterfeited); the sequence is intercut with flash-forwarded images of the sexual act's residue, as the two figures dress again, to leave the room and enter the city. The inclusion of this sequence in the film indicates the precarious relationship with corporeal and political dissent which such images still carried at the time; all that lives on in the suffocating film city, voided of any trace of the recent European upheavals, is sex. The two actors too remain stylistically marked – in clothing and hairstyle, and via their public reputations as dissidents – by that now-fatigued counter-culture and its conflictual rapport with the film's present moment. The explicitness of the sequence transmits a momentary vision of the social impact of the '60s sexual culture into the world of the film, but that revelation serves only to reinforce the latter's despondent tone and preoccupation with figuring death. The film's sexual puncture-point remains transitory; the menacing city re-exerts its grip, and those two ecstatic bodies, convulsed by orgasm, vanish.

Don't Look Now views the city as a hostile and enveloping presence, effortlessly capable of swamping any resurgence of the corporeal ignition which had made the 1960s an exceptional moment, both for the city and for film. Roeg's film helped to determine a caustic but passive approach to the power structures of urban space during the remainder of the 1970s and into the subsequent decade. Although a few European cities were still intermittently struck by the impact of dissidence and opposition, those forces most visibly took the form of mediatized terrorist acts. Few film-makers (the West German director Rainer Werner Fassbinder being a prominent exception, with his 1979 film *The Third Generation* and his contribution to the collaborative film *Germany in Autumn*, made in the previous year), possessed the audacity to create filmic confrontations with those determined acts of urban violence – which manifested themselves as bombings and kidnappings – and to probe those acts' intimate rapport with the transformed dynamics and representations of sexual acts. Subdued by the reverberations of the previous decade, the film city of the 1970s became a zone of careful sensory exploration within which individual figures in transit resisted being engulfed while tentatively examining their wounded memories and attempting to formulate untainted futures.

The film which most embodies that catalepsy of the film city is the Swiss director Alain Tanner's *In the White City* (1983), in which the enclosing hills and alleyways of Lisbon provide asylum for an exhausted sailor who abruptly abandons his ship; for the entirety of the film, set over several months, the nameless sailor wanders around the city, stares at its façades and calmly searches for an explanation for his descent into immobility, uncovering nothing. In a parallel way, the film recounts almost no incidents: at one point, the sailor is nonchalantly robbed and later confronts his attacker, and, almost by chance, he enters into a tenuous relationship with the chambermaid of his dilapidated hotel; otherwise, the city's time and space expand around his figure in its solitude. His corporeal presence gradually seeps into the buildings around him, so that he finds himself vulnerable to the city's caprices; this city possesses little of the malevolence of Roeg's Venice, but it blithely disregards the sailor and deflects his fragile interrogations, so that he dissolves ever further into its surfaces. That gradual crumbling of the corporeal into the urban ultimately becomes painful, taking the form of a dissolution into alcohol and anger, and the silent dialogue of sensory loss and disappearance pursued between the sailor and the city finally generates the need to escape back to the sea.

Throughout the film, the sailor obsessively films the façades of Lisbon and his own face with a small super-8 camera. The reels of undeveloped film are packaged up and posted to his wife in an anonymous city in land-locked Switzerland. The sailor declares to his wife that he has now lost the capacity for words and can only reach her through images. The woman is shown projecting the films to herself, in her solitude, watching the exultant face of the sailor (in images shot by himself, at arm's length) after he deserts his ship and begins to film panoramas of the illuminated city, scanning its decrepit buildings and its children's wildly running figures. Subsequently, though, the super-8 films no longer hold the face of the sailor, who has vanished too completely into the city's layers to invoke images of his own body, and only captures the city's surfaces and the water of the estuary, maladroitly shot from trams and ferries. Those fractured sequences, incorporated into the narrative, create vivid gaps within its otherwise homogeneous form, projecting the gradual dissolution of the sailor's vision while also penetrating the matter of the city which adheres him to it. The film's linear narrative itself eventually disintegrates, relying increasingly upon the super-8 images to seize the essential, minor upheavals in the sailor's world, until even those images give out. On his escape from the city, the sailor must sell his film camera in order to generate the funds for a destination-less journey; at the start of that journey, in the film's final shot, the face of a young woman filmed in super-8 on a train reveals that the sailor has regained the capacity to conjure his own images.

As in many of the city films of the 1970s and early '80s, the time of the city in Tanner's film is that of an aimless waiting, experienced in solitude and silence. The sailor immerses himself in the infinite act of staring at the city, both by day and by night, and the film's only temporal indicator is the unease articulated by the hotel's proprietor over whether the sailor will be able to pay his inexorably mounting bill. Lisbon too exudes a lack of time: the façades of its alleyways have already eroded to such an extent that the process of

In the White City, Alain Tanner

decomposition is impossible to gauge, and human movements focus around archaic gestures of transaction. The
city's inhabitants resist any sense of urgency, habitually
lounging in cafés or idly riding around on clanging trams,
maintaining a blithe approach to the passing of their lives.
Lisbon, in its filmic apparition of 1983, remains poised in a
strange temporal zone beyond the edge of corporate Europe,
and the use of super-8 film stock (already almost obsolete at
that point) as the principal visual medium for rendering the
city serves to propel its time even further into stasis.

The sailor's endless journeys through Lisbon on foot
expose him to the city's excessive space; his body remains
perpetually submerged within that void, ambivalent space,
which exerts no intrusive power on its inhabitants but also
provides no cohering framework for their lives. While the
sailor's focus narrows to an ever denser point in his search to
discover an object for his gaze within the city, that space
expands simultaneously, opening out into glaring panoramas
of white light and dust. Lisbon's landscape maintains the
capacity of the sailor's body to exist in flux, but restricts it to
continuous circlings of identically contorted alleyways.
Although the Tagus estuary forms a prominent presence, inti-
mating escape via the close proximity of the ocean, it is mostly
screened from the sailor, hidden away behind the minuscule
detail that extends across the buildings' innumerable graffitied façades. Gradually, that luminescent city space presses
too heavily on the sailor's perception, which collapses down
into a few raw, essential elements; confined in darkness in his

bare hotel room, he finally becomes aware that he has to engender his own space.

In the city films of this period, itinerant characters often subsist in a state of suspension, attempting to block the visual force of memory – above all, the exacting cultural memory of the 1960s upheavals, but also the immediate memory of the present moment, which insistently demands a re-imagining of the city and of the body's status within it. Although the sailor of *In the White City* jumps ship ostensibly to repair his ruined memory and thereby envisage a tenable way into the future, few active presences of memory actually manifest themselves in the city's drained space. He remembers to send his super-8 film reels to his wife, but the nature of memory itself comes increasingly unstuck. In an earlier film of interminable urban wandering, Wim Wenders's *Kings of the Road* (1976), a repairer of obsolete film projectors and his companion travel in a van along the border between West and East Germany, from cinema to cinema, from location to location, strategically opposing the onset of memory. The characters' greatest desire is for blissful forgetfulness within which the wounding imperatives of urban existence could be perpetually dissolved. The film image itself forms the vital medium for exploring the abandonment of memory in the city.

The revitalization of the European film city came at the end of the 1980s, with the vast transformation of the continent's borders, power structures and visual dynamics. Those upheavals led to the sudden collapse of media systems that had

held supremacy for 40 years; Eastern European film industries
– such as that of East Germany, which had intricately examined the post-war urban landscapes of Berlin, especially the
status of its female inhabitants – disappeared overnight. The
film cities of the decade's end became infused with seminal
images of turmoil and revolution, each carrying a distinctive
sensory charge. Although images of exultant cities predomi-
nated in the first months of that period of chaos, the engulfing
changes soon produced more ambivalent responses, as entire
sections of urban populations were thrown into positions of
economic vulnerability. Film images of the city's inhabitants
captured the altered status of the human body, articulating the
elements both of potential and of shock which that time
contained. Certainly, the kinds of images endlessly explored
over the preceding years, of morose figures marooned in indif-
ferent cities, evanesced instantly; now, images of elated human
masses resurged into film for the first time since the street riots
of the late 1960s. Individual lives on the urban periphery also
became vital material for young film-makers who sought, often
with grandiose aspirations, to recreate the city.

By far the most ambitious of the fictional city films of
that moment, Leos Carax's *Les Amants du Pont-Neuf* (released
in 1991, but in production since 1987, its protracted evolution
absorbing all of the period's upheavals), probes the city's layers
of detritus as well as its more lavish dimensions. In its narrative of two marginal figures who meet while sleeping rough in
the middle of Paris, on a medieval bridge long closed off for
renovation, the film interrogates both the city's undersides

and its void centre. The images catch hidden and subterranean elements in the form of urban spaces invented or overhauled by the film. In its first images, the male character, Alex, is maimed by a car while staggering drunk along a boulevard at night, and is then jammed into a police bus with other unwanted or obsolete inhabitants of the city and dispatched over its edge, to a clinic for homeless alcoholics in the suburb of Nanterre. In his dereliction, Alex becomes so absorbed by internal corporeal pressure that he can no longer use language; his body is evoked instead by violent images of urban shattering. The film's female character, Michèle, also suffers corporeal and visual disintegration in the form of a degenerative eye disease. While living together on the abandoned bridge, they witness a spectacular visual eruption (Paris's Bicentennial celebration of 1989, which in the film encompasses all of the diverse urban uproars of that period). The two characters accord themselves an absolute freedom to disregard every visual and territorial boundary of the city, but their volatile relationship – continuously jarred by perceptual and bodily malfunctions – can only adhere through their vision of the city in flux around them.

The Pont-Neuf allows Alex and Michèle to view the city from a distance, since the bridge has been barricaded in order to be renovated. It forms a unique space in the city: the point of origin for a challenge to Paris, as well as an endangering zone that incessantly provokes the two protagonists to intensify the brief time in which they can inhabit it. Carax had intended to shoot the entirety of his film on the actual

Les Amants du Pont-Neuf,
Leos Carax

Pont-Neuf, but following a delay caused by an injury to the actor playing Alex, Denis Lavant, the period Carax had been allotted in which to use the bridge expired. He was forced, at enormous expense, to construct a replica of it and of the façades of the buildings alongside it, in a quarry in the south of France. The Situationist philosopher Guy Debord, in a documentary film made shortly before his death, viewed Carax's bastardized city as indicative of the denuding of Paris by its visual media, and as corruptly signalling the terminal point of any sense of the city's authenticity. Eventually, when the shooting was over, Carax's duplicated Paris had to be abandoned to the elements; he was aware of the aberrance of his hugely extravagant city, but perceived its re-creation of Paris within a framework of criminality rather than of legitimacy: 'In some way it was the trace of a crime that had to be erased, but the crime was a beautiful one'.[1]

Whenever they are seen outside the space of the city, the human figures of *Les Amants du Pont-Neuf* form a collection of wracked and lost bodies, attempting to maintain their balance as they experience the dizziness of lust or the desire for alcohol and barbiturates. In one sequence, the character Alex is seen spitting petrol-fuelled fire from his mouth while turning precarious somersaults. Extracted from the city, the body exposes itself to an imminent plummet into empty space. In the sequences filmed in the Nanterre clinic for destitute alcoholics, shot in a documentary style within over-illuminated rooms, the emaciated bodies are rendered in bleached images of scarred, tattooed flesh; the figures often lose their balance and abruptly fall to the ground, against a clamorous sound-track of cries and insults. The body must be placed in juxtaposition with the city's cohering space in order to exist.

The film ends with a final fall of the body, as Alex and Michèle accidentally plunge off the bridge and into the river – a fall which they barely survive, and which precipitates their departure from what they ultimately come to see as an accursed city. Carax's Paris comprised such a space of intense transmutation that it was to prove impossible to replicate; it took him eight years to complete another film, *Pola X*, saturated, in its narrative of a Bosnian refugee's journey to France to find her brother, with intimations of the burnt-out and bombed cities of 1940s and '90s Europe, rather than the exhilarated cities of the end of the '80s. *Pola X* moves to the suburbs of Paris, siting itself within a terrain of dilapidated industrial warehouses, and the film's few journeys into the city engender only calamities for its human figures.

Among the many visual transformations undergone by European cities in recent decades, the changing status of London remains a mystery. Within the perceptual configurations of urban Europe, London projects a void zone that exudes multiply detailed and compelling visual and corporeal elements to its spectators. London pre-eminently generates images from its densely inscribed, profusely filmed urban space, and the assembling of all of its filmic representations might elude even the infinity of a digital archive. Images of London are more uniquely captured at a tangent, from filmic

journeys across its face which can seize and explore the fractured substance of its urban memory and volatile sensory
resonances. But London also forms a European city maxi-
mally adept at rendering even the most contemporary images
immediately obsolete. In two experimental films from 1993,
Patrick Keiller's *London* and John Maybury's *Remembrance of
Things Fast*, the insensible rapidity of London's evolution
works to erode the images made of it and expose the fluctuating matter of memory.

In its narrative of two invisible, abrasive male characters endlessly traversing the city on foot, from the peripheries
to the centre and back again, Keiller's *London* probes the
permanent fascination and repulsion of its urban textures.
The film's narrative traces are carried by its disabused voice-
over, which gently excoriates the city, occasionally uncovering
precious images or sites among the sprawling dereliction and
squalor. The city's very mutation provides valuable source
material for the travellers' obsessions: since the film depicts
London as an integrally absent, even disappearing, presence,
the harsh process of that evanescence itself can serve momentarily to grip or grate the eye. The nameless narrator and his
companion, Robinson, combat the redundancy of their own
eccentric re-imagining of London by gathering data about the
city's exiles, especially its resident nineteenth-century French
poets, above all Rimbaud, whose often unintentional or solitary habitations are tracked down to crumbling or already
demolished buildings. Apart from those moments of subdued
revelation, the film forms a corrosive observation of the city's

London, Patrick Keiller

political and social power structures, deploying a glacial eye and advanced irony on the 'annus horribilis', 1992. The film ends with a conflagration as the travellers attend a vast bonfire, with the figures of the city's inhabitants tenaciously outlined against the flames.

London scans its way across a raw urban landscape whose substance resists being easily caught or encompassed. In the lengthy period of the film's shooting, the film-maker and his few collaborators found themselves often abused or assaulted, subject to sudden hostilities, as they filmed along-side fume-clogged roads or at the boundaries of London's regimented corporate terrains. That landscape is often one of homogeneity, from the Tesco and Ikea surfaces of the obliter-ating suburbs to the architecture of infinitely replicated office complexes, hastily erected during the late-1980s property boom. The film's pre-eminent evidence of the city's violently inflected layering comes with the royal unveiling of a statue to Arthur 'Bomber' Harris, instigator of the wartime bombing raids on Dresden and Cologne, and a principal architect of Europe's destroyed cities of 1945; London exudes a belligerent presence even within what are ostensibly its most publicly sanctioned sites. And it forms a partially ruined set of awry façades, still irregularly shaped from its own wartime damage and, more immediately, from the IRA bombing campaign which exacts a uniform level of devastation on its slapdash corporate towers. The further the film tracks its way into London, the more urgent becomes the need, however deep its futility, to castigate the city's systems of power. And ultimately, the film's own process of visualizing the city is imbued with solitude and intimations of peril, its salutary recreation of its unwilling subject executed against the urban grain, at both visual and corporeal risk.

John Maybury's film *Remembrance of Things Fast* – with its Proustian title and its primary concern with the city's sexual dimensions – exists in unsteady counterpoint to Keiller's film of the same year, but both excavate the fragile nature of memory under the visual impact of London. Maybury's project was to map the city through evocations of its gay culture in the Thatcher years, inserting himself into the frame as both a sexual and a remembering participant. His intricate visual memory of London is structured as an oblique interior dialogue between himself and his film, in a profoundly fragmented and tentative form, rather than via the definitive, exterior images of Keiller's film. But Maybury, too, depicts a vanished or evanescing London, its tenuous survival emphasized by the film's rapidly splintered montage of human voices and figures, each of whom narrates a particular memory of their arrival or experiences. Surrounding those individual, conflictual memories – focusing on elements of the exhilaration or subjugation engendered by contact with the city – the film constructs a vertiginous digital imagescape composed of terrorist figures, inane media newscasters and illuminated urban façades. In its confrontational response to London's repressive form during the Thatcher era, Maybury's sense of nostalgia for London and for its seminal acts is explicitly positioned in spite of the city itself.

In such films of London, the incessantly vanishing city carries an aura of being able to oppose its own portrayal with malicious determination, thereby exacerbating the mystery of its contemporary visual status. The city possesses the capacity to defuse, as archaic, all images or languages made of it – not through its own ongoing architectural metamorphoses (as with a city such as Tokyo), but via a more strategic resistance to images. On London's flaking, decrepit façades, the hold of images soon appears anachronistic. Nothing becomes more rapidly archaic than a surpassed digital technology, and Maybury's visual memory of the city, shot in part on near-obsolete super-8 film and then digitally remixed, is lost in its own vanished contemporaneity. Keiller's own strategy proved more perversely astute, since he shot his film with an Eclair Cameflex (a film camera closely associated with the French 'New Wave' film-makers at the end of the 1950s), intentionally infusing a pre-emptive archaism into his resonant images. In their exploratory attempt to grasp the matter and memory

Remembrance of Things Fast,
John Maybury

of London, the two films also serve to prefigure future images of it. In both films, London is perceived as being situated at the end of the world – an urban space that can be viewed with clarity only from within the trajectory of an outward journey of one kind or another. However, both film-makers do not finally travel far from their city; in Maybury's film, the terminal point is a suicide attempt, from which he reawakens back in the city, while Keiller's abandonment of London at the end of his film forms only the suspension of a locked visual fascination.

Contemporary Europe's urban cinema increasingly projects an overpowering compulsion to explore and create city spaces exterior to the continent's ostensible parameters, which increasingly encompass a fractured and dissolved presence, its visual forms homogenized by corporate media and tainted by political and national forces. The dereliction of Europe, exacerbated by its digital cultures, has been experienced by film-makers as necessitating excursions outside it, especially to Japan, the US and North Africa, to engender hybrid images of amalgamated cities, able to propel their spectators' eyes simultaneously in all directions, thereby revealing Europe's precarious visual status. The supplanting media images that have deadened Europe's historical layers incite a filmic response in the generation of vital urban spaces that exist in caustic opposition to those desolate zones of digital media. The void terrains of European cities now function as empty screens, their own ephemeral content of advertising images too rapidly exchanged ever to cohere in their spectators' eyes, and so pre-eminently capable of launching more demanding perceptual journeys into the disintegrating matter of memory. The future of European urban culture comprises both a loss and a crucial meshing of cities, whereby film-makers may engender visions, often wrenching or painful, that extend far beyond Europe's now-redundant confines and fabricated limits.

Claire Denis' 1999 film *Beau Travail*, which epitomizes that vivid search of memory for images both exterior and integral to Europe's cities, situates itself in Marseilles, using the narrative device of the Foreign Legion to convey an insurgent corporeal force that effortlessly crosses borders, visually surpassing Europe; Denis' reinvention of the Foreign Legion metamorphoses her group of displaced male figures into sexually inflected presences who spend their time executing strenuous choreographic gestures of confrontation on mountains overlooking the ocean. In Marseilles, a pre-eminent city of exile (often defined in the French media as the 'dustbin' of Europe), a former Legionnaire, Galoup, expelled in disgrace for planning the death of a member of his platoon, becomes immersed in his damaged memories of the landscapes of Djibouti, at the far eastern edge of North Africa. Galoup – played by Denis Lavant, a decade on from Carax's *Les Amants du Pont-Neuf* – drifts through his post-Legion afterlife in desolate municipal housing, and his aimless journeys in solitude and desperation through the illuminated concrete panoramas of Marseilles induce both memory and narration. His cursory voice-over notes: 'My story is simple,' and that laconic narration often lapses into total silence, allowing the film's evocation of European memory to become saturated by painful, intricate images, propelled backwards and forwards between the now-alien urban space of Europe and of Djibouti. At the film's close, Galoup is about to commit suicide in his bleak room, but even in his final moment, he remains involuntarily compelled by memory; his body itself remembers, as the rhythmic beating of an arm muscle sends the film out from Europe, seamlessly back to Djibouti's cacophonic nightclubs.

The city outside Europe which forms the locus of memory in the film is rendered as an unsteady concoction of visual materials from multiple sources: the dilapidated urban space of Djibouti, marked by the commercial insignia of the US (the walls are dense with tin hoardings for Coca-Cola and Sprite), is also inhabited by military forces originating from Europe, who implant their visual and sonic cultures into the city. The nightclub of Galoup's final recollection constitutes

Beau Travail, Claire Denis

the sensory core of that urban space, which precipitates him into a delirious but solitary dance. However, the film locates the seminal site of Djibouti far from the city, during the sequences in which the young Legionnaires are summarily dispatched to a spectacular, deserted mountain terrain of salt-lakes and volcanoes, where they develop their new corporeal freedom. That overwhelming landscape, painfully extracted by memory and sited between the two divergent urban landscapes, within and outside Europe, re-defines and transforms those cities.

In another film by a female director, from the preceding year, Yolande Zauberman's *Clubbed to Death*, the location is the visually mutating zone at the city's edge. A young woman falls asleep on a bus in Paris and abruptly awakens at the urban periphery, within an uncertain wasteland of abandoned buildings utilized as techno-music nightclubs, whose sensory attraction soon engulfs her. These zonal landscapes, filmed in the suburbs of French and Portugese cities but evocative too of the edges of North African cities, oscillate between the peripheries of Paris and those of other cities that are interconnected in their desolation. As in Vertov's *The Man with the Movie Camera*, the components of the film city are assembled from different spatial origins in order to construct a distinctive city which, in Zauberman's film, is poised between European and extra-European space, especially infused by the visual cultures of North Africa and demonstrating a style of film-making that determinedly exits from the city's central corporate domain. In such works, prescient of the future of urban cinema, both the film's characters and its spectators remain lost at the farthest point of the European city and are compelled to visualize their own way back in or out.

The rapport across post-war European history between the city and the film image is uniquely intimate and conflictual: the medium of film insistently seized and projected all of the period's upheavals of urban life and their multiple impacts on cities' inhabitants. Often aberrant spaces, the film cities of Europe explored the continent's volatile existence and memory, revealed shifts in the power of its media and societies, and scanned transformations within the technology of the image. European film-makers now increasingly interrogate the very form of Europe, often perceiving its cities as existing in a process of erosion or disappearance, along with the corporeal status of their inhabitants; that sense of disappearance, though evocative of the dominance of digital corporate culture, also serves to make urban boundaries evanesce, provoking film-makers to probe the zones between cities and continents, and between the image and the human body.

3 japan: the image of the city

The contemporary film image of the city possesses an itinerant dimension which – as in Claire Denis' *Beau Travail* – can revealingly carry it across contrary film cultures and divergent cities, from one side of the world to the other, its visual layers historically constructed and enlivened by decades of conflictual rapports and power struggles between continents, countries and cities. Film forms the pre-eminent medium for a traversal between cities, from one urban panorama to another, and from one architectural nuance to another: the visions generated by such unexpected leaps into the urban unknown have always provided cinema with one of its most compelling traits. The ambivalent fascination of those movements, via the medium of cinema, from European cities to other ones is perhaps encompassed most incisively by films which suddenly emerge from their trajectory into Japanese cities, especially Tokyo. That endless oscillation of the film image, forwards and backwards through urban space, has both imposed European preoccupations on Tokyo's visual surfaces and allowed Tokyo to function as an unwilling, deviant screen for the reflection into Europe of insights into matters of sex, memory and death within the urban arena. As contemporary Japanese urban culture increasingly surpasses and negates that of the US in its world-wide influence, Tokyo – of all cities beyond Europe – carries and projects a unique filmic, sensory captivation.

Andrey Tarkovsky's 1972 science-fiction epic *Solaris* begins with a sequence in which two astronauts, Kelvin and Berton, meet at the isolated country house of the former's father. Kelvin is about to be sent to a space station that orbits the distant Solaris, a turbulent planet with an aberrant capacity to generate hallucinations and to mirror the most intimate desires of its human observers. Kelvin must decide whether the potentially dangerous mission is worth pursuing. Berton shows him footage of his own, calamitous journey to Solaris and subsequent interrogation by space-programme bureaucrats. After the screening, the two astronauts quarrel over the nature of Solaris in the otherwise noiseless gardens, and Berton abruptly leaves in his car, before calming down and making a telepresence call (a call accompanied by a film image of himself, although no camera recording or transmitting that image is discernible) to Kelvin, with the image of Berton in his car appearing on the same screen on which the film of Solaris had been viewed. Inexplicably, Berton is now transported to Tokyo: from the silent outer-space landscape of Solaris and the rural landscape of Kelvin's house, the film suddenly launches itself out onto the cacophonous motorway overpasses and under-passes that cross the city's dense landscape.

Berton announces that he is calling from 'the town', but the city of the astronauts is never identified. In a sequence lasting for five minutes, but possessing such a hypnotic visual impact that it seems to extend indefinitely, *Solaris* captures Tokyo's startling urban terrain, filmed through the windscreen of Berton's car (although the texture of the image intimates that the human figure and the city actually exist in two different spatial dimensions, with Berton in his car filmed in a Moscow studio). As time passes, the journey moves under- and above ground, via darkened underpasses armatured in concrete and overpasses that generate panoramas of the surrounding, vividly inscribed edifices. Occasionally, the steady momentum of that interminable urban journey is broken by shots of the pensive human figure at the wheel of the car. The film image itself mutates, enigmatically passing from black-and-white to glaring colour, while the sound-track intensifies, gradually reinforcing its amalgam of distorted traffic noise and scrambled radio frequencies. The image only ever registers the city's surfaces. Towards the end of the sequence, the soundscape accumulates to a jarring level, and the image fractures suddenly; from its linear journey across the city's visual carapace, it suddenly ascends to a static viewpoint far above the concentrated grid of seething motorway junctions, framing them in such a way that the two principal arteries traverse one another in an 'X', as though marking a summary cancellation of the coruscating surface. Then, that infinite apparition of Tokyo vanishes, and the film returns to the deep silence of Kelvin's garden.

Solaris, Andrey Tarkovsky

Tarkovsky experienced considerable difficulty and delay in obtaining permission to leave the Soviet Union in order to render Tokyo as his astronauts' city, a 'town of the future' as he envisaged it. He clearly prefigured the city's space as one that would counter any visual trace of Europe while emanating the hallucinatory or alien resonances he desired. After briefly filming in the city around the end of September 1971, he wrote in his diary: 'Japan is a wonderful country, of course. Nothing in common with Europe or America. Tokyo is an amazing city. There's not a single factory chimney, not a single house that looks like any other.'[1] In its transformation for the filmic world of *Solaris*, Tokyo is vitally connected to Europe by its defining dissimilarity – a dissimilarity that characterizes its own constituent elements. But in that process of imposed re-invention, it also becomes a visually suffocated city, intended to exist uniquely within the film's conception of urban space. Impossible to penetrate or incorporate, the city constitutes a kind of galactic black hole within the film, whose gaze can only scan those resistant urban surfaces.

Even within the constricted role accorded to it in *Solaris*, Tokyo activates an exploration of the matter of memory in the city. In the telepresence call which he makes to Kelvin, Berton insists that Kelvin must experience an unleashing of memory when he travels into space and sees Solaris from the space station. He presciently warns Kelvin that viewing Solaris will uncover lost figures from his past. From that perspective, the film's vision of Tokyo appears as a residual hallucination from Berton's own journey to Solaris, in the form of a terrifying memory that remains active. Tokyo's virulent urban surface is made, involuntarily, to perform as a kind of disruptive screen for memory, which is generated from that surface in the form of a series of images that accumulate towards their own breakdown or disappearance. The presence of Tokyo evanesces from the film once it has served that enduring use. And the entirety of Tarkovsky's film works to engender images that can function as urban and corporeal manifestations of the workings of memory.

In the French film-maker Chris Marker's 1982 essay-film of Tokyo viewed from Europe, *Sunless*, the city appears in an inverse image from that captured and enclosed by Tarkovsky a decade earlier. Marker lovingly rips the city open, exploring its visual layers and relating everything he sees back to Europe – and then out again from Europe to further, disparate urban landscapes, especially those of West Africa. The film slips from city to city, from image to image, from body to body, infinitely permutating those three seminal components. Marker renders Tokyo's visual elements as existing in a constant state of oscillation, infusing them with both delicate and violent interactions. Whereas Tarkovsky tracked Tokyo's unidentified surfaces from the suspended heights of its over-passes, never arriving and never leaving, Marker adopts the more habitual transport mode of the city film, arriving by train and then restlessly excavating the city's subterranean dimensions. But he employs an almost identical sonic evocation of the city, accompanying his images with a sound-track of synthesized interferences and distorted voices. Marker probes another dimension of Tokyo's undersides in the form of its hallucinatory media landscapes, placing his images of exteriors against the interior, nocturnal terrain of sex and violence carried in unending ocular impacts from his television. For Marker, the Japanese-language narration explicating those media images is incomprehensible, making the news

Sunless, Chris Marker

reports he watches of Europe (in particular, the upheavals in Polish cities around the end of 1981) revealingly opaque, inciting a relentless, imaginary re-creation of their content. Marker views Tokyo's inhabitants as being subjected to exhausting obsessions by those media images, and he juxtaposes them with his own images – outlandishly blurred by primitive computer technology – so that the city dissolves into its essential forms in figures of conflict.

In its journeys across and through the space of Tokyo, *Sunless* occasionally coheres around images of the city to which Marker perceived himself to be individually attached: the hypnotic street-dancing of the Awa Odori festival, or the Gotokuji temple devoted to the city's cats. Tokyo is envisaged as an alien but intimate terrain whose resonances are often cinematic: it forms a B-movie 'Planet Mongo' of spectacular but disregarded architectural constructions and peripheral, searched-out banalities. In filming the vast image-screens of the Shinjuku department stores' façades and the minute, rhythmic gestures of the city's inhabitants, Marker performs an engaged visual anatomization of the city rather than an imposition of Europe onto its surfaces; his film is able to move freely outwards from Tokyo whenever a compelling association unexpectedly dispatches it. Suddenly, the film shifts through time and space to Iceland; the rationale for that leap unravels only gradually and enigmatically. That abrupt transition also motivates another film of urban movement, Fridrik Thór Fridriksson's *Cold Fever* (1994), in which a reluctant Tokyo fish salesman is instructed by his grandfather to travel to Iceland in order to perform death rituals for his parents, who died years earlier on a geological expedition. The uprooted Japanese figure, lost within the darkened urban space and snow-covered volcanic landscapes of Iceland (another geologically unstable island that strongly fascinates the Japanese), mirrors Marker's unseen cameraman adrift in Tokyo, struggling to connect its impenetrable forms to his own perceptions and memories.

Almost all of the images of Tokyo in *Sunless* become incorporated within its ambivalent investigation into the perpetual question of memory; Marker attempts to discover memory within the film's networks and webs of time, or to find it pinioned between his images' capricious spatial transformations. Memory is conjured too through the counterpositioning of images with the film's voice-over, in which a woman recites extracts from letters sent to her by the itinerant cameraman whose images (like those of Vertov's 'man with the movie camera') simultaneously invent the city and constitute the film. But memory remains a resistant matter, always ready to slip away between image and text, between space and time. In its maladroitly computerized images – their forms generated with intentional archaism – the film finds a medium at least to prefigure the fundamental loss of memory. And when memories allow themselves to be caught, within the film's fragile, interstitial urban substance, Marker recognizes that they are only memories of memory, from which the original content has long seeped out to become lodged elsewhere, within the endless memory archives of the city's surfaces. Concurrently, the film's journey aims to obliterate memory by entering a structureless void, and exists too provisionally for memory to survive. Tokyo, with its uniquely precarious urban configuration, forms the supreme site for that wilful destruction of memory.

Marker's film emphasizes the element of self-destructive violence in Japanese culture and the ways in which that compulsion becomes mediated through Tokyo's urban space; in that ostensibly innocuous city, violence remains imminently, seismically present, its traces most discernible in the form of its film culture, both in historical cinema and in contemporary horror, sex and gangster films. From his European perspective, Marker views Tokyo as a collective but flawed space of dreaming, always edged with calamity. In an essay accompanying a book of his photographs of Tokyo, *Le Dépays*, published at the same time that *Sunless* appeared, Marker writes:

Once violence is unleashed, disorder is everywhere – it cannot satisfy itself with the law of an eye for an eye, and every idea of justice or reparation is dismissed; violence can only end by engulfing itself, like a volcano . . . The most disturbing thing about Japan is that you get the impression that the imagination is in conflict with itself – that the imagination has a double form, and in the end it is impossible to exorcize the violence of the world via the spectacle of the dream; instead, a conflict takes place within the space of the dream, and the fate of the world itself is at stake in the spectacle of that conflict.[2]

Whereas outbreaks of violence in European cities habitually result from direct confrontations between nations or individual figures, they must operate more tangentially in Tokyo, moving without transition from imagination to urban reality, from dream to act, with that capacity for sudden insurgency further exacerbated by the city's proven vulnerability to ruination from earthquakes and other subterranean forces.

In his invention and opening out of the space of Tokyo for *Sunless*, Marker constructs what is clearly his own urban survival zone; even with its emanation of inexorable violence and its location at the other end of the world from Europe, Tokyo provides Marker with what he intimates is a 'home' and with the memories (or, at least, the memories of memories) that he desires. He incorporates footage, shot a decade or so earlier, from his participation in the fierce protests surrounding the building of Tokyo's Narita airport, the images of warring protesters and riot police resonating with those of the riots that took place in European cities, especially Paris, during the same period. And even beyond the exhaustive visual cataloguing that forms Marker's positioning of Tokyo against and within Europe for *Sunless*, film history interconnects Tokyo and European cities in the form of other upheavals. In particular, the film image of the fire-bombed, vanished Tokyo of 1945 allies itself with that of Berlin and other European cities from that moment. But even so, the post-war history of Tokyo and of its film images remains exceptional, carrying an acute sensory aberrance that makes it finally resistant to amalgamation with urban images of Europe.

In Tokyo's post-war history, film images explore every surface of the city, in which urban and corporeal obsessions are tightly bound together. The incorporation of the city by film images helped to shape its volatile spaces and visual styles from the moment of its disappearance in 1945, through the American occupation and subsequent decades of tumult and corporate elevation, to the crashed form of contemporary times. Film tracked a compulsive chain reaction of urban acts and dreams, whose images were projected in cinema spaces before the entranced eyes of the population. Caught in Tokyo's dense urban landscape, its inhabitants were propelled headlong through the city's transformations (often moving simultaneously forwards and backwards), and viewed film images as the instilling of calm and silence within agitated lives, or of furore and anger within routine ones. Film came to possess a salutary, contrary force, repositioning bodies and rearranging urban elements. Through the channelling medium of the film image, the eye could construct an individual sense of distance from the vivid horrors of city existence. But with the onset of the digital image throughout the urban space of Tokyo – its power increasing at the same time as the city's corporate structures started to collapse – new and potentially shattering implications began to emerge for the body within the city, in the form of infinitely void images drained of corporeal substance.

During the American occupation of 1945–52, an idiosyncratic regime of censorship imposed itself on Japanese cinema, fluctuating especially around the representation of labour unions and the status of Communist groups in the re-emergent country. Under that censorship, the ruinous state of Japan's cities was rarely shown, and no authorization was accorded to films depicting the militarism either of the country's feudal or its recent history (such as that of its brutal colonial expansions of the 1930s). The pre-eminent film images, contained in the occupiers' preferred genres – the contemporary family melodrama, above all – were of resilient figures enduring the hardship which the incineration of their city had brought on their heads; when Tokyo itself was shown, it was as the flattened zero-terrain of debris through which processions of determined figures advanced, carrying innocuous banners exclaiming their intention to rebuild and revivify the city. The American film-maker and writer Donald Richie arrived in Tokyo for the first time in 1946; in February 1947, he described the view from the central Ginza crossing in his journal: 'I stand and watch the mountain fade. From this crossing it had not been seen since Edo times; but now all the buildings in between are cinders. Between me and Fuji is a burned wasteland, a vast and blackened plain where a city had once stood.'3 That landscape of urban and human ashes, irreparably mixed together, proved to be of seminal importance for the city's film images.

By the end of the 1950s, with the occupation over, those earnest processions had turned to ferocious demonstrations against the enduring military power of the US in Japan, the protests captured in newsreel films as great assault waves of human figures swarming around the Tokyo parliament building. The first fiction films of Nagisa Oshima, from that delirium-edged moment, show the strategic refusals of Tokyo's young inhabitants. The city's avenues became the vital site of those protests, but they extended into the city's subterranea, where a culture of experimental film-making developed alongside innovations in choreography, performance and visual art. The destruction of Tokyo had brought with it a deep sense of exhilaration for those of its surviving inhabitants who had been in their teenage years at the time, and that exhilaration transmitted itself into a vibrant culture of meshed sexual experimentation and revolutionary aspiration. The city's sexual uproar was focused especially in the eastern-Shinjuku district, which grew during the 1960s in an explosion of multi-storey, high-rise sex complexes. The face of the city metamorphosed, bearing the conflictual influence of American culture and, increasingly, of European cultures – especially that of France – on its surfaces as well as within its cultural undersides. Yasujiro Ozu's final films, from the beginning of the 1960s, depict the marooned human elements of a now-frenzied city, still attempting to maintain their zones of stillness, but caught within the immense sense of melancholy projected by the neon-illuminated night city. The building of a spectacular motorway system in advance of the 1964 Olympic Games helped to consolidate film images of Tokyo as the world's 'future city' (as Tarkovsky certainly perceived it to be); those images scanned urban spaces transformed by the ascendant economy, its financial proliferation embodied by the endless 'salary-man' work force of compressed commuters. But in the final moments of the 1960s and the beginning of the following decade, the city went haywire once again, its avenues ripped by the cacophony of vast, violent protests against the continued subjugation of Japan to the US, that eruption of anger exacerbated still further by the use of areas around Tokyo as American air bases in the Vietnam War.

The corporate, technological Tokyo which grew in prominence from the early 1970s led to an evanescing of all limits to architectural ambition, resulting in a supremely aberrant urban space compounded from every strand of world architecture together with a high degree of hallucination. Tokyo expanded its space further and further, spraying out its commuter-dormitory suburbs to the west, so that they voraciously engulfed other cities such as Yokohama. In many film images of the city from that period, its former dissident elements, now mired in lassitude, have been exiled to the most dilapidated districts, while the vast suburban work force – in such films as Sogo Ishii's *Crazy Family* (1984) – endures an existence of glaring, incessant insanity. A colossal industry of pornographic film and other visual media grew around the necessity of sensorially sedating that work force, both during its commuter journeys and in its precious moments of leisure. The future of Tokyo depended on the city's capacity to maintain a maximum momentum, in both its corporeal and its urban dimensions. But the corporate excess of the city's business conglomerates, with their lavish dissipation of income and networks of corrupt political alliance, finally precipitated the crash of 1998.

Contemporary Tokyo carries the residue of that economic exhaustion, both in its human population and in its pinnacled landscape of grandiose, vacant buildings, arranged in avenues still virulently imprinted with the insignia of collapsed international technology conglomerates. In Tokyo's culture, the human body is thrown into relief by that dissolution of corporate power, but it is an urban body perceived simultaneously as endangered by exterior forces and as the origin of unstoppable mutation and horror; the body's intimacy with the digital image (its corporate content now emptied out) creates unsteady amalgams of corporeal and visual elements, within which the film image maintains a deteriorated, but still obstinate, presence. The sense of a terminal fall of the city and its suburbs resonates with the images of both Japanese and European cities in 1945, while the ritualized confrontations of contemporary protesters – focused on media and ecological concerns rather than on political or revolutionary upheavals – serve to evoke, in the interdependence of their opposed contestants, the film images of Tokyo's 1960s street battles. But in Tokyo, the carapace of history soon falls away, and only the raw matter of the image remains.

Among the infinite images of Tokyo, those of Seijun Suzuki's film *Tokyo Drifter* (1966) carry the deepest sense of prescience about the city's visual future. The film, with its elliptical, involved perception of urban space, renders the city in revelatory but shattered images. Although made as a generic product (framed as a gangster film) for a Japanese studio, Nikkatsu Corporation, *Tokyo Drifter* remains a resistantly bizarre and individual visualization. Suzuki's turbulent directing career, marked by disputes with the studio, was almost over by the time he made the film; largely neglected in subsequent decades, he reappeared almost 30 years later to play the old man who instructs his salary-man grandson to travel to Iceland in Fridriksson's *Cold Fever*. Suzuki's own film contains imperative images of Tokyo, seized within the moment of its transformations and inflected with a determination to impart to the city a crucial, contradictory charge of desolation and elation.

The opening sequence of *Tokyo Drifter* forms a condensation of city space into the essential material of its visual and sensory components. The first images are those of a bleak railway yard, filmed in such bleached exposure that the saturated white light predominates over the figure of the gangster Tetsu, moving towards the spectator. To the contemporary eye, habituated to images veering freely across the space and time of history, the shots of stationary wagons irresistibly evoke the railway yards of concentration-camp Europe, but for a spectator in the 1960s, they would have presented a peripheral, uneasy terrain of dilapidated dockland, whose vacancy invited the intrusion of violence. The passive Tetsu is viciously beaten by members of a rival gang and left beside the water, his body barely distinguishable from the ground on which he sprawls. The void city continues to exist above his unconscious form, emitting minuscule gestures and traces of industrial noise around a core of silence. Slowly, Tetsu gets to his feet, supporting himself between two railway wagons. Finally, his passivity breaks open, and the unleashing of his fury materializes the city in the form of a sequence of Tokyo cityscapes. The city metamorphoses from black-and-white to colour images in the moment of that revivification. Those images show the 'new' Tokyo, recently reconstructed for the 1964 Olympic Games, each image propelling another one forward: the Tokyo Tower (over which the film's title is superimposed), the railway station, the motorway overpasses (which would soon prove so compelling for

Tokyo Drifter, Seijun Suzuki

Tarkovsky), the Olympic swimming-pool, the bridge over the Sumida River, Hibiya park and, finally, a glowing night neonscape of the high-rise buildings surrounding the Ginza crossing, from where Richie had, twenty years earlier, viewed the vanished city. That abrupt traversal constitutes a compacting of body and city between human sensory desperation and luminous urban façades that generates a fundamental sense of precariousness.

An equally unprecedented film, shot in that same dockland terrain and allied to Suzuki's film in the fragility accorded to Tokyo's urban landscapes, had been made four years earlier by the young experimental film-maker Takahiko Iimura. Where Suzuki's film was a studio-funded project intended for cinema audiences, Iimura's super-8 film *Junk* had an inverse financial basis, having been made without money and for no immediately apparent audience. *Junk* scans elements of an eroded, virtually disappeared city in its images of the intersection between the urban and the marine, at the edge of Tokyo's harbour. The city is composed of its own detritus: dead animals, decaying consumer objects jettisoned into liquid mud, and human figures scavenging or fighting with one another. Iimura uses a cacophonous soundtrack to exacerbate the effects of his images (as in the films of Marker and Tarkovsky, the city appears to demand acute sonic distortion as its correct accompaniment, here accentuated to painful levels). Both Suzuki and Iimura adopt a corrosive approach to narration in their images of Tokyo: Suzuki scrambles and warps the multiple layers of his ironic gangster narrative, while Iimura gradually accelerates his images of decay into a pure narrative of death. For Iimura, the form of Tokyo is that of an open arena for visual re-creation, especially within the marginal zones. His retrospective view of *Junk* and of its memory of Tokyo diverges in its sobriety from the exhilarated nihilism with which he had originally shot his film:

Junk, Takahiko Iimura

The beach of Tokyo Bay was a dumpsite for all of the city's human, animal and industrial wastes when I shot *Junk* there in the early 1960s … From today's point of view, the film certainly shows concern with ecology and may be regarded as an early attempt to deal with the destruction of our environment.[4]

Any concern with ecological issues had been almost unknown in the parallel universe of early-1960s Tokyo, the receptacle of a determined governmental effort to augment levels of urban pollution and blight within the shortest possible timeframe. But Iimura's reinvented memory of the city, channelled via his uniquely open images, possesses the capacity to become identical with the images and obsessions of the contemporary moment.

Sex exists only at an amoebal level in Iimura's film, but in *Tokyo Drifter*, it determines the entire stylization of the city. The film's pervasive emanation of sexual uproar collects within the space of a nightclub, its exteriors agitated in neon gestures against the darkness (as with the urban surfaces of *Zazie in the Métro*), while its lurid interior is regulated by a relentless sexual frenzy. Tetsu is the sole inhabitant of the film city who refuses to participate in that sexual regime; determined to embody a total loyalty to his gang boss, he exclaims: 'I'm off women' and declines all requests for sex, including those from European women, that would detract from his concentration. Like a contemporary inhabitant of Tokyo, immersed within its digital culture, Tetsu avoids the hazardous sensory black-outs and entanglements of sex in order to move fluidly across the city's screens and façades. He forms the only aberrant component within its sexual space, which extends seamlessly from the film's images into the cultural and social chaos of mid-1960s Tokyo, whose political acts alone are excluded from the film. Even when Tetsu becomes aware that his boss has repudiated him, his conduct still annuls the city's sexual sway, since his itinerant life of solitude as a 'Tokyo drifter' precludes even the momentary congealing of a sexual act.

At the end of *Tokyo Drifter*, Tetsu kills almost every one of the other characters, even his boss, in a retributive rage that clearly compensates for any sexual abstinence; he then disappears into the city's visual web, walking away from the spectator in the reverse direction to his first appearance in the railway yard. That final scene of killing forms virtually the only coherent narrative sequence in the entire film, which habitually proceeds obliquely in its cursory tracking of curtailed or barely perceived actions. *Tokyo Drifter* moves immediately between neural and visual flashpoints, thereby projecting the volatile matter of Tokyo directly into the film. As in many contemporary depictions of urban space, the city's elements are assembled only by intensifying the range of their sensorial impacts and via a wry abuse of, or oblivion directed at, linear narration. The temporal dimension of *Tokyo Drifter* carries the precariousness which the film transmits to the city: once that film city has fleetingly burned itself into its spectator's eye, it can only evanesce, leaving behind a few preposterous florescent traces.

The moment of *Tokyo Drifter* saw an escalation in the binding together of Tokyo's revolutionary and sexual obsessions with the city's surfaces. Although protesters had staged violent demonstrations around Tokyo's centres of governmental power since the end of the 1950s, the last few years of the 1960s became fractured with increasingly ferocious riots, often staged in the avenues of Shinjuku; at the same time, the riots and sexual experiments began to disintegrate as they reached the far boundaries of governmental and corporeal flexibility. The aspiration towards revolution among Tokyo's young population allied itself to some degree with the other waves of urban tumult from that period, taking on much of the iconography of May 1968 in Paris and of the South American guerrilla movements, but Tokyo finally remained obstinately isolated from the radical projects developing with diverse degrees of success in Europe and the Americas. Tokyo's visual culture of revolution and sex retained the element of a performance undertaken in an inescapable city that would maintain its permanent rhythm of urban mutation, however much the insurgent gestures of violence and sex might exacerbate the fragility of its transformations. In part, the uproar and the degeneration into disabused lassitude of late-1960s Tokyo was infused with the still tangible destruction of the city, two decades or so earlier, which arbitrarily negated all urban ambition, but that uproar also possessed a unique character in the preeminence accorded to the visual image in tracking the gestures which mediated the city's dimensions of affront, ecstasy and violence. As a result, every event and act lost its own disparate status and became transmitted entirely into those collective images of chaos which overruled individual memory and created a definitive visual memorialization of the revolutionary, sexual city.

In newsreel and television images of the Shinjuku riots, the intricate motivations and inspirations for the protests immediately leak out. All that remains is the corporeal rush of running figures, all clearly marked with their allegiance – the police with their shields and uniforms, the protesters with their slogan-inscribed helmets and masks; both factions maintain a high degree of organization, the combat taking place within the city's avenues in co-ordinated charges and counter-offensives. Even so, the battles emanate a sense of primary disorder, only superficially segmented into zones of discipline. And when lost stragglers fall at the feet of the riot police, any sense of discipline vanishes in the face of vicious baton blows to their heads. The filmed figures bleed profusely. A fictional annex to the television images of street conflicts, in films of the period, took the form of oblivious inhabitants of Tokyo descending the stairways of their apartment blocks to find bloodied protesters sprawled before them, confronting them with the dilemma of ignoring or helping the damaged figures. Such images of violence became a source of deep fascination for the Japanese population, watching news bulletins in which they became irretrievably meshed with that moment's other images of world-wide conflict, from Vietnam to Prague. The Shinjuku events were propelled a world away from the city through the mediation of those grainy black-and-white images, opaquely flickering from television screens. The isolation of the images for Tokyo's inhabitants became reinforced still further when they showed battles taking place in the countryside, where one focus was on opposing the construction of Narita airport. The choreographed displays of intense violence between vast gatherings of protesters and riot-police resonated more with fiction-film epics of Japan's twelfth-century military turmoil than with events taking place in intimate spatial and temporal proximity. Those images collapsed, too, to the primordial form of human bodies being beaten by figures of authority. Even when experimental film-makers shot footage of the same riots, it retained that intractable quality of futility.

In Tokyo's sex images at the end of the 1960s, rendered through pornographic and experimental films, and also through photography, the basement drinking clubs of Shinjuku form the site for corporeal amalgams of ecstatic figures. Mouths open to their maximum capacity in convulsions of orgasm; bodies are sent askew by sexual seizures. The Tokyo pornographic film industry expanded relentlessly at that time, its momentum allowing film-makers working at its peripheries to use sex as their means to generate images of the city in a state of sensory and revolutionary crisis. The pornographer most preoccupied with grafting together the subject matters of sex and revolution in his films, Koji Wakamatsu, often filmed narratives entirely consisting of sexual acts within small groups of urban revolutionaries, in hiding from the police or from their own factional commanders, sprawled across minuscule tatami-mat rooms in the moribund suburbs; exhausted by sex and pitched between elation and lassitude, they generate the impetus only at the last moment of the narrative to perform a terrorist act, blowing up a hijacked plane or assassinating a governmental or corporate figure. Wakamatsu temporarily broke off his film-making in 1971 to involve himself with Palestinian terrorist organizations. Film and photographic images of transvestism, transsexuality and gay sex all formed crucial elements in the reinvention of Tokyo's sexual iconography, with the city's densely inscribed surfaces integrally positioned. In Shinjuku, the span of corporeal experimentation moved seamlessly from the fierce riots taking place on the district's avenues to the sexual acts executed – often with a parallel degree of violence – within its subterranean spaces. In film images, the body ephemerally encompassed both the intensified content of sex and the demands of that moment for revolutionary upheavals to be enacted, above all, on the face of the city.

The cultural residue of that unique period took the form of a body of experimentation that linked film-making with styles of performance, especially choreography. Figures such as Shuji Terayama and Tatsumi Hijikata were able to channel the corporeal furore of the period into their creative work. The fractured insurgency of the moment had allowed a number of influences from Europe to become especially strong, particularly that of Jean Genet – whose novels evoke an urban atmosphere of gay sex, criminality and transvestism that proved seminal within Tokyo – and of Artaud, who had called in his final writings and radio broadcasts for revolutionary upheavals within the human anatomy. Japanese film-makers' work at the end of the 1960s became crucially inflected with the parallel preoccupations with urban revolution and sex in the work of such European film-makers as Godard and Fassbinder, but their exposure to such works remained too intermittent and partial to submerge their own distinctive style; the imageries of European film culture became meshed as one visual source into Japanese urban cinema together with elements drawn from Japan's historical cultures of sexuality and of resistance to dictatorial and exploitative power. Similarly, the disruptively surreal element in many Japanese films of that moment drew productively on the far peripheries of European literary Surrealism, especially on the work of Georges Bataille, but avoided assimilation by the movement's doctrinaire core (from both a sense of independence and a relative absence of documentation, Japan's own Dadaist and Surrealist movements of earlier decades had also taken only those elements from their faraway European counterparts that enabled them to confront their own urban and sexual obsessions). The engagement in Tokyo with the international artistic and filmic arena was only narrowly reciprocated. Many of the city's artists and film-makers became exasperated with its cultural isolation and its newly ascendant corporate power, and exiled themselves to other cities, especially New York and West Berlin (although they often eventually returned to Tokyo). With the onset of the 1970s, the ferocious moment of urban aberration in Shinjuku dissipated as rapidly as it had begun, with terrible implications for those of its participants who could neither adapt themselves to the corporate city nor transpose their anger and sensory excess into images.

All of the boundaries of power and physicality that appeared so tangible and obstructive for late-1960s Tokyo – definitively stalling its dual obsession with sex and revolution – now form entirely obsolete presences within the city's contemporary digital culture, where the nature of memory itself mutates. Participants of the Shinjuku street riots remember and evoke a simultaneity of cacophony and silence, of calm and violence – but the sensory dimension is diluted within a collective memory of that tumultuous city as having disappeared, with many of its participants expelled to suburban or languorous zones of decay. Archival television-news footage of the riots centres on the police charges and on the intensity of the violence, from which the original sexual resonances have evanesced along with the protests' political imperatives. As a result, memory becomes drained of focus, entranced only by void movements and the desire for collectivity in the act of remembering. However, Tokyo's contemporary surface itself remains perversely archaic as a screen for memory, that deviance only accentuated by the incessant turnover of rapidly annulled digital images.

The film that engaged most with that intricate, often violent rapport between revolution and sex was Toshio Matsumoto's *Funeral Parade of Roses* (1969). By the time the film was shot, the determined belief in revolution which had sustained the riotous inhabitants of Shinjuku was rapidly disintegrating; the film's exhausted figures still adopt the iconography and visual stylization of urban revolutionaries, but they have lost all tangible connection with their city. The sexual focus of *Funeral Parade of Roses* is on the transvestite culture of Shinjuku, but the film also takes a mythic turn into more deadly sexual experimentation, in the form of an incestuous relationship that leads to the suicide and self-blinding of its two principal characters. The sexual acts in Matsumoto's film are played out against a backdrop of street riots, but those corporeal assaults are screened away from the film's own characters, despite their often voiced aspirations towards revolution. The riots are seen only as television footage watched by the characters, or as film images within the film; those characters never directly take part in the riots. Instead, the film itself suffers damage, in the form of solarizations and scratchings of its celluloid. *Funeral Parade of Roses* presents a cityscape in vibrant transformation, fuelled largely by elation and ecstasy, and manifesting itself in physical and visual rhythms of orgies, wild bouts of dancing and communal film screenings. By its end, that film city has become saturated in desperation, its final image posing a bloody knife in useless threat against Tokyo's oblivious façades.

The film's emphasis on the corporeal is carried by the camera's relentless tracking over the naked body and often orgasmic face of the transvestite Eddie, as he engages in acts of anal sex with the other characters, including his own father and the most spurious of the film's gang of inept young revolutionaries, 'Guevara'. Eddie (played by the actor Peter, best known for his role as the Fool in Akira Kurosawa's 1985 film *Ran*) spends much of his time wandering aimlessly through the Shinjuku streets, accentuating the film's fascination with probing the tension between physical and urban surfaces. Eddie's body also projects the ambivalence accorded to sexual flesh by the film: the body may be the potential point of origin for unleashed acts of revolution, but it also forms a zone of endured subjugation – Eddie is perpetually under the sexual control of the film's other characters, who nonchalantly pass him around among themselves, and he moves across a contrary urban landscape of lacerated and murdered bodies set against ecstatic and orgasmic ones. In that film city, with its axis in the vulnerable human figure, the only channel through which to elude Tokyo's corrosive power structures is to vanish into the white heat of orgasm, or else to metamorphose sexually, via the intermediation of the film's volatile imageries, into resonant forms like that of the rose.

The rose metaphor intimates the source for much of the film's sexual obsession and iconography: the novels of Jean Genet. Both the film's title and its principal location – the 'Genet' transvestite bar in Shinjuku – betray its infatuation with that work (an infatuation shared, as we have seen, by many of Tokyo's artists and film-makers at that time, including Nagisa Oshima, who had made his Genet-derived film *Diary of a Shinjuku Thief* in the previous year). The appropriation of images of deviant, urban sexualities from Genet's work was exacerbated by a preoccupation among Tokyo's visual artists with the aura of criminality – Genet had written his first novel while imprisoned for theft in Paris – and by attempts to infuse artworks and films with the same sense of intensive social provocation which Genet had imparted to his

Funeral Parade of Roses,
Toshio Matsumoto

novels of the early 1940s, resulting in censorship and outrage in France. The seminal presence of Genet's work in the subterranean visual culture of late-1960s Tokyo had a strange counterpart in its exterior space; by coincidence, Genet spent several weeks visiting a lover in Tokyo in 1969, the year when *Funeral Parade of Roses* was made, and took part in a violent Shinjuku demonstration, though he determinedly avoided all contact with Tokyo's cultural figures during his stay there.

Tokyo itself possesses an endangered, precarious status in *Funeral Parade of Roses*. It forms a cursed, archaic terrain of death, as well as a compellingly visual arena for vital acts of sex and revolution. In a sequence set in a cemetery at the funeral of a transvestite suicide, Eddie watches in horror as vast areas of waterlogged tombs slowly submerge, and exclaims that he wishes that Tokyo, and the entirety of Japan, would sink beneath the ocean without trace. Tokyo is an elusive site that can only be touched by exposing the body to its acts of violence; the gang of young revolutionaries surrounding Eddie avoids that raw contact, preferring the city to be mediated by its images. Rather than go out into the hazardous city, they gather in a cramped tatami-mat room and use a super-8 camera to film the misshapen images of the Shinjuku riots as they are transmitted on a news broadcast from a malfunctioning television set. In triumph, they then screen the resulting distorted images to themselves, as though the accumulation and viewing of images in itself constitutes a revolutionary act. The corporeal distance from the city unfolds in layer upon layer of media images that paralyse active participation in the upheavals while simultaneously inciting a sense of euphoria. The revolutionaries' elation precipitates a furore of naked dancing and then an orgy, the film images disintegrating into scrambled human forms crammed between the thin walls of their room. As with almost every film of Tokyo at its moments of insurgency or metamorphosis, *Funeral Parade of Roses* juxtaposes its visual content with a cacophony, the sonic impacts grating against the images of sexually frenzied bodies. When the somnolent revolutionaries finally emerge into the city, that space intimates only vacancy and death, traversed by hearses and the staggering figures of injured rioters, its façades flooded with advertising hoardings.

Funeral Parade of Roses is itself immersed in images of death, which culminate in its final, horrifying scene of violent suicide and self-blinding. Film, throughout its history the superlative medium for figuring death, generates a unique meshing of death, visual perception and the city in Matsumoto's provocative work. Its images remain deeply engraved within the substance of contemporary Tokyo, emanating both a malediction against the city whose brutally insidious power stopped the most ambitious social protests of its post-war decades in their tracks, and also an ambivalent celebration of its aberrant sensory and physical textures. The film's images of death are invariably edged with ecstasy (in the same way that Genet's language is an evocative mix of lethal curses and orgasmic gasps), thereby preparing a prescient visual concoction for Tokyo's mutating urban surfaces and corporeal forms.

Tokyo's contemporary cinematic preoccupation with the corporeal as an integrally precarious matter exists in direct rapport with film images of the city itself. Rendered in film, that city forms an unhinged and unliveable space; although the works of the 1960s film-makers remain vital as sources of provocation and nostalgia, urban space is now defined through negation rather than via the potential for revolution or ecstasy. The flaws that collapse the city are not all of its own making: they carry the historical residue of disparate but enduring variants of Tokyo that disappeared from the same site – the city flattened by the great earthquake of 1923, or that incinerated by the firestorms of 1945. Those virtual, destroyed cities inflect the contemporary one as phantom presences. More intimate to the present than those city-wide

calamities, the assaults on parts of Tokyo by religious or apoc-
alyptic cults (especially the Aum Shinrikyo gas-poisoning
attack on the subway system in 1995) infuse the place with the
potential for its population to be randomly decimated. And at
the immediate, corporeal level, the city's over-concentration,
which requires but obstructs daily mass-commuting traver-
sals, has its central axis in banal and pressurized corporate and
educational environments that intermittently incite explosions of psychosis, resulting in suicide or the small-scale
massacre of groups of inhabitants, particularly school-chil-
dren. Above all, Tokyo's saturated urban media environment,
with its infinitely renewed bank of consumer images, generates perpetual overload in the responses it exacts from its
inhabitants.

Faced with the near-impossibility of representing the
amplitude of that urban meltdown, contemporary films of
Tokyo often possess an interchangeable appearance, narrowed
down to homogeneous elements of alienation. But the films of
the director Takashi Miike such as *Audition* (1999) supplement that depiction with an excavation of the ways in which
its human figures are also sexually endangered. Miike's film
narratives are sexually driven – his Shinjuku-based characters
have often performed a multitude of sexual acts, especially
anal or murderous sex, even before the films' opening titles
appear – and seek to examine the implications of a pervasive
misrecognition of corporeal identity in the city, which can be
scanned most vividly within the fractures of sex. In Miike's
characters, perception has become too distorted or distracted

by the city's visual imperatives for it to focus on individual nuances of identity; as a result, those figures inhabit spaces of hallucination in which they are forcibly accorded an ultimate liberty of action. With its corrosive approach towards Tokyo's all-powerful visual façades, Miike's aberrant film world is one in which the malfunctions in perception induced by contact with the city can overturn every aspect of sexuality, abruptly reversing tenderness and violence, freedom and subjugation. Film sex in contemporary Tokyo no longer carries the aura of experimentation and defiance which it held in late-1960s films such as those of Matsumoto; it forms a more tainted, often obliterating presence that mirrors the urban surfaces within which it is pinioned.

The loss of a monopoly over images of the human body in the city, which film and photography had possessed overwhelmingly in the 1960s, propels disconnected corporeal elements at high velocity across Tokyo's urban media. In its defection from film, the image of the body becomes absorbed by more mobile technologies, adapted to the imperatives of contemporary viewing conditions, in the form of transmutating images on hand-held, pornography-generating computers or on the displays of cellular telephones, feverishly manipulated by commuters on their endless journeys through the city. The bulky manga pornographic comic books, still comfortingly brandished by 'salary-men' at the end of the 1990s, are now increasingly being superseded by digital, minuscule images of bodies in animated sexual convulsions. The radical diminution of the contemporary corporeal image

exists in sharp contrast to its previous status, projected onto
the screens of the city's cinemas, where the viewing of its life-
size form in glowing darkness ensured a sheltered, captivating
experience for its spectators. As in many city centres across
Europe, the large-scale disappearance of cinema screens from
Tokyo has exacerbated its inhabitants' difficulty in erecting
their own individual screens to insulate themselves away from
the abrasive urban arena (in the way that the young revolutionaries of *Funeral Parade of Roses* were able to protect themselves from the Shinjuku riots by cocooning themselves in
their room and watching those riots as drained, refracted
images). The end of the ability to view the film image of the
body cinematically within urban space itself constitutes one
more opening for the city to intrude on the precariously
screened perception of its inhabitants in transit. Contemporary Tokyo exacts a compulsory sensory participation in its
corporate visual surfaces and with its corporeal images in a
vital but subjugating strategy of imposition.

The dilution of cinema as the medium used to interrogate the urban forms of Tokyo – a social questioning at work
since the period of the American occupation, particularly in
documentary cinema – has had the result of reducing the city
to caricatures of its most striking architectural elements: the
vast government towers of western Shinjuku and the department-store terrains of Shibuya. Tokyo becomes diminished
to an abbreviated sequence of images (like those which
Suzuki used in *Tokyo Drifter* to embody the 'new' city of the
mid-1960s) whose grandiose architectural priorities demand

the neglect of its peripheral or subterranean spaces, with their escalating dilemmas of poverty and exclusion. In those zones of authoritarian prohibition, the contemporary figures of marginal Tokyo pursue lives at acute variance with those of its central spaces. The film image of Tokyo, over the post-war decades, gathered the textures of the entire city into visual forms that demonstrated the ambivalence and capricious power on which the city based itself. But the digital image of the city necessarily focuses on its pivotal corporate sites, and the increasingly supplanted film imageries of the peripheries appear obsolescent within that glacial visual system. Those marginal and suburban parts of Tokyo still maintain their presence, however, in the work of photographers such as Nobuyoshi Araki, where the sexual, deviant charge integral to such peripheral sites disrupts the city's more homogeneous spaces.

Above all, it is the obsession with corporeal mutation which constitutes the essential element in the contemporary filmic iconography of Tokyo. In seminal films from the late 1980s and early '90s by the directors Shinya Tsukamoto (creator of the two *Tetsuo* films of 1989 and 1991) and Sogo Ishii, the terrifying metamorphosis of salary-man figures into concoctions of lacerated flesh and technological debris evoke the fundamental human rip within the urban matter of transforming, corporate Tokyo, then at the short-lived zenith of its affluence. The corroded residue of the city's void technological culture becomes meshed with unique, feral anatomical components in images that themselves carry extravagant mutations, in the form of abrupt temporal contractions, damaged celluloid frames and intensive ocular shocks. Those film images resonate with documentary footage of the wounds and irrevocable corporeal alteration suffered by the victims of nuclear radiation and industrial pollution, from Hiroshima and Minamata, and also with the monster films of the post-war decades (especially those centring on Godzilla, driven to gratuitous rage by atomic contamination). But in the Tokyo of headlong corporate ascendancy, the monstrous filmic body determinedly transmitted its fury at technological power into urban space, with that spectacularly mutating form engaged in a direct, irresoluble combat against the surfaces of the city.

Shinya Tsukamoto's film of corporeal mutation, *Tokyo Fist* (1995), opens with a disembodied arm posed against the backdrop of a Shinjuku corporate tower, its fist clenched in fury against the city. As with the image of the bloodied knife raised against a Tokyo façade which closes Matsumoto's *Funeral Parade of Roses*, the image of the arm is accorded the capacity to project an act of physical opposition or dissidence into urban space. In Tokyo's contemporary films of the body, the spectator becomes immersed in a unique ocular dynamic, by which the eye is compelled to scan the image at high speed, to accustom itself to a rhythm of visceral jolts (and always to anticipate the next collision), and to construct a sensory rapport with the filmed body in its state of upheaval. Such demands on the eye imply a commitment on the part of the spectator to interrogate the raw substance of the city and its corporeal implications. In *Tokyo Fist*, the spectator's eye even penetrates flesh, forced through the disintegrating material of bodies that have suffered the impacts of the city or of blows aimed by its warring characters. In that film city of perpetual visual and neural shocks, human figures endure corporeal seisms as they relentlessly traverse urban space, moving from one confrontation to another. That visual upending of the body is accentuated by a sonic cacophony of the kind which has had an enduring presence in films of Tokyo for a period of four decades; but *Tokyo Fist* adds layers both of corporeal noise (crashes of bone on bone, soundscapes of malfunctioning internal organs, vocal cries) and of relentless traffic and other urban noise to that sound-track, so that the city becomes sonically mediated through the bodies and urban acts of the film's characters. Night images of the landscapes of western Shinjuku – the zone of colossal corporate headquarters and high-rise government buildings – work as rapid puncture points within the film's narrative, determining both the characters' and spectators' responses to the violent meshing of city and body.

Tokyo Fist generates its sparse narrative traces into dense sequences of sex and combat, leaving no space whatsoever for reflection, in a parallel form to Tokyo's saturated spatial structure, designed similarly to excise all questioning of its arbitrary assembling of urban and human elements. The film's visual sequences constitute such an intensive and immediate ocular experience that they necessarily evanesce

Tokyo Fist, Shinya Tsukamoto

entirely at the end, with the result that the spectator is compelled subsequently to individually revivify those images, which then themselves mutate into provocative hallucinations of the film's opposed urban and physical forms. *Tokyo Fist*'s fragile narrative concerns a near-catatonic insurance sales-man, Tsuda, who is taunted and sexually humiliated by a boxer whom he had known at school; the brutal boxer attracts the salesman's fiancée, Hizuru, that compulsion manifesting

itself in her self-piercing of her nipples and the inscription of tattoos onto her body. Tsuda (played by Shinya Tsukamoto himself) begins to train in a gymnasium in order to reinforce his body for future reprisals against the boxer, but his efforts only result in grotesque corporeal deformations that expel jets of blood. The three interlocked characters incessantly attempt to subjugate one another, their futile strategies positioned within the city's overarching power of subjugation, caught by the film in images and cacophonies of exhausted human masses engaged in endless commuting journeys. In Tsukamoto's film city, all sexual acts have their axis in humiliation and violence, and the city's rapport with its inhabitants is explicitly rendered as sexual in its obliterating control over human life. The only memories that can survive in that environment are of death.

The sole positive narrative outcome of *Tokyo Fist*'s urban frenzy is that Hizuru's physical transformations, indelibly engraved into her flesh, serve to propel her away from the catastrophe embodied by Tsuda's salary-man existence, which he blankly reassumes at the end of the film; her future remains open. Otherwise, Tsukamoto's vision of contemporary existence in Tokyo takes a relentlessly caustic form: the film's cityscapes show vast, empty corporate towers, illuminated at night, while their human components are contained into the minuscule, flickering images of surveillance cameras or blindly perform their insane corporeal floods of movement across the opaque, screeching terrain. The film accentuates the perpetual degradation that results from the volatile meshing of the city's physical elements into its corporate structures. That degradation incites the film's visual delirium, in its horror at the city's sensory engulfing of its inhabitants, whose forms dissolve, disappear and resurge. The film's final images are of blurred, broken faces set against the city.

In the visualization of Tokyo in post-war cinema, the city undergoes immense upheaval, both in the forms and strategies of the films which render its urban space and within the city's surface itself as it is exhaustively probed and transformed by those images. The medium of film, sensitized to movements in urban and corporeal matter, and to shifts in the nature of memory itself, tracked the multiple history of the human figure in Tokyo, contrarily encompassing both its revolutionary and its subjugated bodies. The most vital film images of Tokyo carried the determination to excavate (or annul) the city's vast sensory domain. In contemporary Tokyo, the forms in flux of the digital image, the human body and the film image together emanate the deeply damaged but exhilarated layers of the precarious city. The erosion of the film image's status coincided with the rise of its digital cityscapes, transmitted pre-eminently from the façades of the city itself, via the immense image-screens of its department stores and corporate advertising zones, and also from the minuscule, hand-held digital screens which contributed to the obsolescence of the city's cinema screens; those digital screens are maintained in intimate proximity to the endangered urban body in transit. But the essential images of Tokyo remain those seized in the films of Matsumoto, Marker and Tsukamoto, which incisively demonstrate to the oblivious city its capacity for insurgence and disappearance.

The historical rapport between film imageries of European and Japanese cities – from the parallel images of vanished, incinerated cities at the end of the Second World War to contemporary images that probe the city's subterranean, sensory spaces and its transmutating corporeal forms – indicates multiple potential ways into the future of visual culture and of the digital city. Many of the images which crucially capture the future of European cities take the form of archaic Japanese films depicting eroded, terminally polluted terrains, such as Iimura's scratched super-8 film of Tokyo's marginal, debris-clogged wastelands. Such images also dissect the crushing impact of the visually saturated, poisoned city on its inhabitants. The immediacy of Europe's future rests on such images, vividly pinioned between history and the contemporary moment, and exhibiting a permanent disabusal with regard to the captivating, void corporate imageries now digitalized by the multinational conglomerates of Europe, Japan and the US. Japan's cinema, above all, presciently explored aberrant, perverse images of the city in disintegration, shot with obstinacy and resistance. The fall of the film image generates a moment of reassessment for the future visual representation of the city, and the essential film images of Japanese and European cities together form points of origin for both confrontations and alliances.

4 the digital city and cinema

In the digital city, the survival of film and of cinema-exhibition spaces forms a contrary element within the engulfing visual processes, constellated with memory and death, that relentlessly configure contemporary urban landscapes together with the bodies and perceptions of their inhabitants. Those spectators of contemporary culture undergo a spectacular and subjugating experience of the eye, the dynamics of which are determined by the city's visual upheavals, which pivot upon cancellation and negation: two forces eminently capable of conjuring a sense of urban ecstasy out of nothing. Although the digital city often defines itself through its own corporate insularity and via an emphasis on its temporal or financial resilience, those visual upheavals necessarily engender a deep split within its substance, so that its urban matter becomes simultaneously adhesive and disintegrative, powerful and evanescent, in its sensory rapport with its inhabitants. The human eye constitutes a vulnerable, unscreened surface, always prone to intolerable intrusion, in its position within a vast network of ostensibly enclosed, homogeneous urban façades; in that process, film forms a kind of archaic ally with the human eye, with its historical capacity to pierce urban surfaces, to unsettle and revolutionize the city.

In its visual form, the city comprises an intricate set of architectural textures and media screens that surround a scattering of obsolete but engrained historical scars. The city's visual façade constitutes its infinitely indefinite and forever surpassed surface-tension skin, a façade whose resilience is amassed and imposed over fragile seismic terrain. The potential for the penetration of acts or images into that visual layer may result from the onset of a sudden calamity or from the riotous insurgence of corporeal elements, provoked beyond endurance by the ecological or corporate arbitrariness which emanates from the city. The residue of catastrophe or of human protest is that of a violent impact on the city's visual face. The presence of the tenacious film image also collides harshly with, and reveals the visual structure of, the city. But film acts in another sense, too: alongside its powerful web of media screens, the digital city is assembled from the delicate visual and emotional projections of its inhabitants, and that often hallucinatory apparition of the city is pre-eminently rendered and narrated in filmic style. The visual compulsions of film enduringly form the primary medium for imagining and annulling the city.

The manifestations of the digital city oscillate between the dominating corporate image-screens which exist to announce its ownership and the minuscule ones which operate in intimate proximity to the body and the eye, provoking intense visual fascination and the blaring vocal texture of exclamation which instantly becomes lost in the city's soundscape. Those external screens are increasingly supplanting any last trace of the city's former cinema spaces. But the city possesses its interior arrangements too, in a domestic channelling and anchoring of its inhabitants within zones of sudden, volatile mutation. The final ambition of digital culture must be the disappearance and replacement of the body, of the city and even of the presence of the visual itself. The status of the contemporary city is based on this contradiction: while saturating urban matter in its rapidly transforming, void content, it also heads inexorably towards its own summary vanishing. Throughout its history, film too constituted an enigma in its rapport with the city, through its unique capacity to focus the eyes of spectators onto projected images that delivered a vast sensory transformation of the urban body and of the city itself. All visual media in the city comprise implosive, paradoxical forces.

The digital city's corporeal forms constitute both the superlative target of its visual manoeuvres and an often strangely ungraspable material, both as contrary, in their diverse ways, as digital culture's power of self-cancellation and film's capacity for contemporary reinvention from a position of technological archaism. However, the primary participant in the strategies of subjugation integral to the life of the contemporary city remains the human eye, with that initial visual hold followed by the gradual engulfing of the inhabitant's entire body. The digital city's variant of Dziga Vertov's massed inhabitants in movement, exhaustively scanned by the film camera, takes the form of a terminally stalled collection of human figures, their pinioned eyes and perception still searching sutured urban façades for a mode of exit for their bodies. But the body itself is more and more overwhelmingly incited by the void process of assimilating and rejecting the contents of these façades: the body becomes ecstatically inundated with sensory resonances and visual attractions that work to bind corporeal substance to the illuminated urban surface. Only the visually self-disassembled body can explore states of resistance to the digital city.

To survey the status of film and of the cinema space in the contemporary city demands a prolonged scrutiny of many urban surfaces: an abrasive cinema journey. Film positioned itself so intractably, often in violent ways, against the forms of twentieth-century urban space – sometimes creating its own film cities in the process – that the digital city and its cinematic residues appear to view one another with mutual hostility. All that remains is to search the city's centre and peripheries for the scattered detritus of film culture and its seminal images, through an immersing visual terrain that has changed insistently and even overturned the status of film. The subterranean experiments of film and the cinematic sites of visual revolution, together with the history of film's self-upending into hilarity or uproar, all exact their enduring presences in the city; by contrast, in the proliferating corporate zones of Europe's multiplex complexes, the would-be spectator finds everything except the traces of film. Such a cinema journey, from its point of departure, often collects not the traces of film images at all, but momentary refractions of digital culture or of human bodies glaringly exposed in disintegrating cityscapes.

I travelled across Europe from its north-eastern to its south-western corners, moving from city to city and entering every cinema I came across. In the course of such a road-movie journey, via urban spaces in turmoil, Europe's vital substance gradually suffuses the eye along with the wrecked or lavish contents of its cinemas. No cinema could be rejected in such a precariously grounded survey, however menacing its clientele or close to extinction its financial regime might have been. Such a journey, through the illuminated night avenues and back streets of European cities, intractably positions itself between the digital and the corporeal, however much it attempts to focus on the cinematic. And the route takes on a zigzag rather than a linear direction, as though following the jaggedly torn outline of a celluloid film frame that had been carried too rapidly through the projector's gate, the image abruptly wrenched from the screen into darkness, the sound synchronization veering wildly into cacophony and then silence. To fulfil the desire to experience the contemporary disintegration and degradation of European film culture and of its spectators' perception requires only the price of a cinema ticket.

That serrated journey through the cinematic landscape of Europe began in Estonia, where admission to one of the country's few surviving cinemas costs a negligible 50 krooni. The vast Stalin-era edifice of the Sõprus cinema stood among the crumbling medieval towers and concrete tenements of

The Sõprus cinema,
Tallinn, Estonia

Tallinn, within a dense urban arrangement of waterlogged
buildings, exhausted human figures and raw corporate placards
(the city's digital screens had so far failed to materialize,
together with the affluence yearned for in the decade or so
following the country's liberation from the USSR). Built in the
late 1940s as a Soviet palace of culture, the Sõprus cinema held
all of its compacted, contrary historical layers on its façade, the
visual evidence of surpassed power still entangled with its more
urgent manifestations: the obsolete hammer-and-sickle
emblems at roof level surmounted a huge carved-granite screen
representing Estonian peasants earnestly harvesting crops,
while the presence of the cinema's simultaneous function as the
'Eldorado' casino and the 'Hollywood' nightclub took the form
of perfunctory illuminated signs on either side of its colon-
naded entrance. Inside the lushly chandeliered but entirely
empty cinema, an anonymous Hollywood thriller, subtitled in
both Russian and Estonian, clanked painfully through the
decrepit projector, its narrative as botched as the projection

itself. The Sõprus formed a tenuously surviving space of cinema in that disabused city, its grandiose surfaces intricately impacting historical memory with the void interval of the contemporary.

I travelled along the Baltic coast to Hamburg and, shortly before dawn, on the peripheries of the Reeperbahn, entered a minuscule subterranean pornography cinema, at the foot of a flight of crushed-velvet stairs. Beneath the alleyways of the frenzied night city, gay pornographic films flickered on the screen while bouts of anal sex were unsteadily executed among the collapsed rows of seating (whereas the seating of the Sõprus had been waterlogged from its terminally leaking roof, here the seats were semen-sodden); cries of orgasm from both the screen and the spectators' space split the dank air. All of that cinema's clientele – the Eastern European prostitutes, the professional consumers of pornography, the pimps and the sailors – would never understand that Europe's cities had ostensibly become 'digital' zones, that their culture had evanesced and vanished: those spectators required only the maximal sensory rush immediately incited by film, until the far end of the night finally swallowed them up. The zeal attached to the history of cinema still held those intent figures in its corporeal grip.

Moving south-eastwards through Germany, via villages whose now-disappeared 'Bioskop' cinema façades of neon had been filmed in the mid-1970s by Wim Wenders for *Kings of the Road*, I bypassed central Berlin and headed for its eastern suburbs. Traversing the near-derelict shopping centre of the concrete-block expanse of Marzahn, I went to an evening screening at the Soyuz cinema, constructed in the 1970s in an architecture complementing that of the suburb (often described in the early 1990s as the most violent place in Europe) at whose edge it was poised. The price of tickets had collapsed to a single euro, and the act of spectatorship itself had become devalued, with a bare scattering of half-hearted participants appearing for the film. The innumerable young participants of Marzahn's only other visual spectacle, its violent 1990s battles between neo-fascist and neo-communist factions, had been lost to alcoholism or consumer stupors. The few elderly and teenaged spectators silently shuffled to their seats, all compulsorily allocated at the very back row of the vast cinema, following some bizarre but unbreakable ritual of distancing spectators from screen that had been established when the cinema had been one of the cultural showcases of the East German state. The final traces of that prestige appeared in the cement murals running along each side of the spacecraft-shaped cinema's screen, depicting interplanetary flight and a fading iconography of heroic astronauts (including that of Sigmund Jahn, East Germany's own astronaut). The spectators sat morosely through the distant Hollywood film, then filed out wordlessly. For a moment, I remained alone in that astronauts' temple, where the disintegration of cinema was occurring in slow motion, in intimate proximity to Europe's most calamitous urban experiment. Marzahn's cinema and its urban space formed dually lacerated surfaces.

Moving westwards to Paris, I looked for the tiny art

The Ursulines cinema, Paris

The Studio 28 cinema, Paris

cinemas at which the Surrealist film-makers had generated their protests and manifestoes, as well as screening their films. Both the Ursulines cinema (where the riotous first showing of Dulac's *The Seashell and the Clergyman* had taken place) and the Studio 28 cinema remained open, largely unchanged from their appearance in the late 1920s; they were rare survivors of that moment's great experiment in cinema, placed in tense rapport with the forms of the city. That survival, in the urban back streets, had resulted from adroitly adapting the films which were shown: the Ursulines had become a cinema specializing in East Asian films, while the Studio 28's façade was now that of an unobtrusive local cinema, its interior sonically convulsed by schoolchildren's screams. But despite those adaptations, the cinemas' riotous auras formed enduring points of filmic volatility within the increasingly oblivious city, still capable of arresting and provoking it.

I travelled on to England, where one of the largest multiplex cinema complexes in Europe had been opened, set among the sprawling commercial zones in the far suburbs of London. Inside, the air stank of rancid meat and stale sugar as the population of that autonomous city endlessly filed down corridors towards the web of minuscule cinema spaces. The time of each film in its unique projection was set in tension with a multiplicity of temporally shifting, ocular demands on those human figures in their state of perpetual transit. The presence of film had become enclosed within a set of impenetrable consumer carapaces, until it formed an ephemeral caprice within that powerful system of attraction and repudiation which focused the eye and body on everything except the film. Everywhere I travelled in Europe, I met identical multiplex architecture and the same blank faces. In those corporate hangars, the stultified populations vacillated between adhering displays of products and fast-food counters, until almost by malign accident they arrived in the rooms where Hollywood films composed almost entirely of digital effects battled in void, self-referential competition with one another, parallel universes away from their spectators. In these brutal multiplexes, the space of cinema stood infinitely removed from its former inhabitation of the city's central boulevards, where it had determined its spectators' intimate visual rapport with that place.

On a Saturday evening, in the centre of Dublin, I walked along O'Connell Street with its line of derelict cinemas. Their colossal façades – their foyers still plastered with posters for their final screenings or for forthcoming attractions that had never arrived, the threadbare carpets littered with drink-cartons and broken chairs – projected the cancellation of the cinematic experience within the city's visual and corporeal arena. In Dublin, the decrepit cinemas appeared not to have been replaced by anything at all; the city's inhabitants milled in seeming fury and loss around that avenue, looking into blaring but deserted amusement arcades or up at the image-screens (themselves already malfunctioning, their exclamations archaic) that surmounted the buildings along the banks of the River Liffey, rawly expelling a cancelled content on the city's visually dissolving space. Around the side of one of the abandoned cinemas, I found an unlocked exit and entered the darkened interior, its ornate ceiling now warped with damp, the rows of ruined balcony seating lying at tangents to one another, the walls virulently graffitied, and everything submerged in a hanging medium of dust. The screen had vanished. All along the avenue, the fused neon signs of the empty cinemas formed glaring gaps of reproach in the face of the city.

From Dublin's collapsed urban space, I flew south to Marseilles. In Dublin, all of the talk had been about an evidently specious economic boom; in Marseilles, it was about death and sex. I headed for the pornography district. In the over-heated stalls of Les Ailes cinema, late in the evening, acts of heterosexual sex took place among the cramped seating, with at least half of the audience facing in the wrong direction; an atmosphere of open-ended compulsion sent pulses of violence into the air. Among that young audience of off-duty Legionnaires and tenement-block teenagers, the regular ritual of the reel change and the interval created by a rip in decades-old celluloid were welcomed; the small gangs of spectators not engaged in the oblivion of sexual acts immediately lapsed into a saliva-expelling cacophony at those almost willed malfunctionings. In such a technologically deficient space, it seemed as though the reels must be held together by a volatile mixture of spit and celluloid (like the original print of Sergei Eisenstein's *Battleship Potemkin* at its first screening), cohered by semen and heat. The cinema space, with its incipient eruptions and technological improvisations, appeared intimately close to the sensory and actual conflagrations of early cinema history. But its site was now that of a last-ditch, residual cinematic Eden.

My journey across the wrecked cinema landscape of Europe reached a point of exhaustion at its far south-western corner, on the avenues of Lisbon. The abrasive collision between body and film image and city that I had witnessed in Marseilles calmed in the lavish interior of Lisbon's one remaining Art Deco film palace, the São Jorge, on the central boulevard, the Avenida da Liberdade. All of the other film palaces now formed gutted, abandoned presences, their grandiose façades rusted or seared by fires. (At least the first-ever cinema built in Lisbon, at the very beginning of the twentieth century, had survived, its space transformed into a sex club where furtive men behind screens eyed Brazilian dancers in their naked contortions.) The visual status of great cinemas situated in pre-eminence within urban space, insistently placing the city's inhabitants in a rapport with (or exclusion from) film for almost all of the twentieth century, was disappearing before my eyes in Lisbon. From the stalls of the São Jorge, in front of its vast, gold-curtained screen, I watched the intricately staged entries and exits of its now-sparse spectators: the little old men in solitude, with their elegant dark suits and hats, and the excited teenagers experiencing a strange exhilaration at their participation in a vanishing but seminal urban act. Then, the cinema darkened suddenly, and the film began.

On a journey across the contemporary terrain of Europe, from end to end and city to city, the surviving traces of film culture surge unexpectedly, often contrarily, through homogenous urban surfaces, revealing their hidden fissures;

simultaneously, the multiplex complexes proliferating around the corporate suburbs configure a meshing of the digital, the filmic and the human into a new, subjugated spectatorial dimension. In their growing dereliction, Europe's cinema spaces comprise zones at odds with the city, edged with corporeal matter: spaces of visual elation and dejection, of memory and oblivion, of sensory nuance and violence. Such a journey across Europe is a disrupted one that scans the status and disintegration of cinema from the position of visual freefall, moving precariously between lost and negated spaces, and between the origins of cinema and its contemporary moment; any film journey now forms an excavation into the history of vision.

From Europe, my film journey took a sudden, jump-cut leap to Japan, as though a flourishing landscape of densely populated cinemas might still be unearthed among its digital cities. Instead, in Tokyo, the dynamics of cinema and city comprised a perverse variant of the forms I had already become familiar with in traversing Europe: the city held a multiplicity of image-screens, but a dearth of film. In Tokyo, even film pornography – still virulent around the visually deviant peripheries of Europe – appeared to have become almost obsolete. The determining rarity of the film image was exacerbated in Tokyo by film's role, over the city's post-war decades, in uniquely interrogating its social structures of power, work and sex. Film now formed a scattered impact of images across and within the city's glaring façades, oscillating between its contrary capacities to confound, to pacify and to instantly overturn an entire system. Among Tokyo's urban, visual and corporeal excesses, film often seemed to constitute the sole scarcity, negated by and revealing the city, both insidious and largely invisible as it manoeuvred its enduring traces through the vulnerable substance of urban space.

In the teeming district of Shibuya, at the very heart of Tokyo's visual and sexual seizure, I came across one of the city's now-rare cinemas, the Rise, accessed via an abrupt descent into a vast basement space, populated almost entirely by an audience of rapt teenaged girls. At the core of the contemporary city, film headed deep underground, in a reversal of the sheerly ascendant forms of the department-store complexes (themselves now reeling into obsolescence with Tokyo's corporate plummettings) which surrounded the Rise's entrance. In that cinema space, the young female spectators kept their eyes locked on the male figures on the screen, occasionally expelling involuntary gasps at their beauty. At the film's end, a team of ushers rushed into place, vocally marshalling the audience to evacuate the space; the human contents of the cinema were strategically tipped out – with a disciplined aberrance akin to that controlling the Soyuz cinema in Marzahn – onto the Shibuya avenues, where a relentless visual combat took place, all day and throughout the night, for pre-eminence over the district's swathes of image-screens. The bodies and faces of Shibuya's inhabitants enacted obsessional, fractured gestures within that digital arena, as though every corporeal act, however infinite its potential replication, stood in permanent danger of evaporating.

Heading northwards into the Shinjuku district of nightclubs, department stores and corporate towers, I entered an urban landscape that had been filmically transformed by the director Takashi Miike into a site of perpetual sexual uproar and capricious explosions of violence. In Miike's rapid-fire cinema, such as his *City of Lost Souls* (2001), Tokyo received a threat that supplemented the wild corporeal mutations inflicted on it by film over the previous decade; Miike's groups of gangsters, invading the city from China and Brazil, irreparably shattered its illusion of national homogeneity. Shinjuku forms Tokyo's most volatile zone; its visual substance – that of both its buildings and its cinema spaces – constitutes an archive of all of the images and presences that negate the city (such as its 1945 firebombing, its 1960s upheavals, its suffocating architectural proliferation and its endlessly torn bodies). The often improvised spaces into which the city's film imageries of ecstasy or ruination still surge are the locations of a subterranean form of vision that compacts riotous images from the late '60s with equally resistant ones generated by contemporary experimental film-makers. For Tokyo's young cinema audiences, late-'60s films such as those of Matsumoto and Wakamatsu appear to come from another world, but arrive in the city with revelatory immediacy; those cinema spaces are saturated in an oblivious nostalgia for such films' projection of turmoil, their audiences tenaciously imagining a new revolution or obliteration for which the entire city appears to plead or lay itself open, from the vulnerable business towers of western Shinjuku to the district's dense webs of digital screens projecting ephemeral consumer images.

Far to the east of Shinjuku, across urban terrains devoid

of the traces of cinema, I arrived among the back-alley film surfaces of the Asakusa district, which determinedly displayed its archaism and refuted the corporate frenzy of the remainder of Tokyo. The entirety of the alleyway that ran alongside the Senso-ji temple had once been lined with film palaces, together with entertainment halls and sex clubs; the few tenuously surviving cinemas of that vanished era now screened a heady concoction of pornography and gangster films for spectators who must have been prone to other kinds of nostalgia, as they watched the images of corporeal penetration or laceration, than that of the young audiences of Shinjuku's experimental-cinema spaces. Even the ticket sellers had been dispensed with, and the elderly men scuttling along the Asakusa alleyway, its walls thickly layered over decades with posters of naked, blood-soaked and tattooed figures, bought their tickets from vending machines outside the cinemas; inside, in glacially empty, muted spaces – an endless Siberian expanse away from the overheated pornography cinemas of Hamburg or Marseilles – the meagre audiences sat in orderly silence while the immense screens above their heads showed orgasming mouths, screaming decap-itations and final displays of insolence in the face of filmic death.

Tokyo, like the cities of Europe, remains vitally inflected, even in its contemporary furore, by its filmic scars, which are densely layered down into its urban surfaces like the Asakusa film posters; only with the extinguishing of the last film image and cinema space could the vast memory and history of the city compacted into film ultimately evanesce. The urban

Film posters in an Asakusa alleyway, Tokyo

and cinematic spaces of Japan and Europe remain uniformly vulnerable to the homogenizing power of digital culture, but each possesses its own resistant strategies or aberrant compulsions that are levelled against that process, the traces of that uneven confrontation being most profoundly at stake – from Tokyo to Tallinn – in the sexual and filmic zones of the city. In the pornography cinemas of Asakusa, I came to the end of my film journey, though that journey could be extended almost infinitely while cinemas gradually fall into ruins or vanish, to be replaced by corporate or multiplex screens or by nothing at all. But such a journey, an exploration of the loss or transformation of vision, would move through a medium of sensory as well as of visual disintegration.

Throughout my journey across the filmic landscapes of Europe and Japan, the overriding presence of pornography manifested itself in its deep entanglement with the cities' digital culture and urban screens. Away from the last-gasp pornographic cinemas of Marseilles and Tokyo, the seminal grip of pornography exerted by the contemporary city engulfs the eyes and senses of its inhabitants: from computer, television and telephone screens, from the printed surfaces of hoardings and magazines, and from the alluring corporate packaging of consumer products. Pornography is inscribed on everything in the city except the body. In digital images of sex, ecstasy itself falls apart, its proliferation pushed beyond representation until it dissolves into a seething mass of indecipherable pixels, then disintegrates still further into banal visual components that can be effortlessly incorporated without distinction into the city's media screens. The faces of the participants of digital pornography become disassembled to anonymity, their corporeal elements blurring into an unrecognizable variant of the contemporary urban body. The relentlessly standardized styles of that pornography traverse divergent cities intact, their imageries rushing from one end of the world to the other, always pivoting on an essential corporeal and ocular subjugation, and channelling the forms of endlessly multiple bodies into one, infinitely extended sexual act.

Of all the cinema spaces I entered across Europe, the pornographic cinemas appeared the most tenacious in their filmic endurance. It often seemed to me that the transmutation of Europe's cities could somehow only be encompassed by the image of a monstrous sexual act, inevitably rendered as pornography, and that the well-worn scattering of pornographic cinemas, invisibly cordoned off from the homogenous city, had been granted a tenuous stay of execution in order to constitute the unique space for that spectacle. Sometimes, the cinemas formed little more than a wretched pit in the ground, signalled by decrepit 1970s neon signs, inhabited by terminally furtive figures, and illuminated by an only intermittently functioning film projector. Those cinemas could just as easily have been cinemas of death rather than sex, like the now-vanished cinema of freezing air and broken-down seating that I once visited at the site of the Sachsenhausen concentration camp: cinemas projecting the barely tolerable film images of Europe's massacres to a transfixed audience. And if death and sex still formed vital matters within the void arena of the digital city, film's ultimate work would be to explore and amalgamate those two elements. In Virginie Despentes and Coralie Trinh Thi's film *Baise-moi* (2000), explicit pornographic sequences intersect with the narrative of a murderous onslaught undertaken by two young women through the peripheral zones of France, from city to city, shooting down or fellating every man they meet. The film was shot on digital video, but was intended for cinema dissemination, so that it strategically pinioned the digital between onrushing cinematic imageries of death and sex. But *Baise-moi*, with its accompanying media furore at the ostensible deviation of its principal director, a celebrated young novelist, into provocative pornography, proved too raw a concoction of death, sex and the digital for both France's

A neon sign and film posters advertising a pornographic cinema, Paris

corporate media systems and its run-down pornographic cinemas, and the film abruptly vanished into the undifferentiated
archive of redundant pornography.

Despite their incapacity to accommodate such films as
Baise-moi, Europe's obstinately surviving pornographic cinemas still seemed to possess their own aberrant potential for an
ultimate outburst at the city's visual core. In those obsolescent
spaces, the celluloid of the pornographic film image was
projected without respite, in a pure repetition and to the most
exhaustive degree, until its substance gradually fell away from
the sexual act which it had desperately tried to hold together
and make immediate, for years or even decades, within its
decomposing medium of Sellotaped rips and tears; that sexual
act then evanesced forever into the humid, darkened air of the

cinema. An accumulated white-noise soundtrack, insistently indented and scratched over time into the flawed celluloid, always accompanied the film's invariable cacophony of sexual cries, together forming a strange mixing of material erosion and the noises of the body. Even at the last instance that a particularly tattered reel could be projected before finally being consigned to oblivion, its fragile imageries retained and transmitted their pre-eminent sensory charge, igniting from frame to frame, from pornographic body to body, as they disintegrated at the same moment as cinema's hold on the city.

Like all of the cinema spaces of Europe, those pornographic cinemas appeared more and more excised from the matter of the city, as though they formed a presence that exceeded, and might even upend, urban space itself. The liquid media of sex that they contained had proved to be at odds with the increasingly desiccated visual surfaces of contemporary Europe, which emanated an essential petrifaction despite the permanently renewed flux of their image-screens. In surveying the incipient dereliction of those sex cinemas, it often seemed as though all of the powerful subjugation exerted by the city had been strategically applied to the space of cinema, until that space (which carried its own, contrary regime of subjugation) had imploded. Any minuscule visual perversion of the digital city had the capacity to decimate its unending corporate homogeneity, dependent as it was on its media's vulnerability to malfunction; as a result, the presence of film pornography, harsh to all of the senses, was being made to disappear in all of its brutal rarity, like some threatened parasitical species that had always been universally despised, but still generated fascination, if only for the moment of its extinction.

On the obverse of that disappearance of cinema, the city staged its own corporate deluge of digital pornography within its avenues and consumer complexes; the digital, in its fundamental intangibility, urgently requires the relentless accumulation of sexual imageries to substitute for its own pre-annulled status. The digital city's media aim at precipitating those pornographic imageries seamlessly into its inhabitants' eyes and into the processes of urban vision itself; that impact possesses the same dynamics of coercion and cruelty previously ascribed to the more volatile forms of cinema pornography, though the contemporary result of these dynamics is a rigorous sensory pacification. The digital city's pornographic surfaces combine with its media strategies until pornography and media together form a single commonplace element within the city's corporate visual power.

In Europe's cities, the forms of media art oscillate compulsively between the digital and the filmic. An obsession with the vanishing of the body and of the city itself, at the core of both media, is configured through deeply divergent strategies. Film possesses its intricate – though relentlessly self-cancelled – history of exploring the nature of urban revolution and corporeal upheaval, alongside which the digital image's preoccupations appear resolutely non-aspirational, engaged primarily with its own status as a medium of power. However, the body remains intimately entangled in both the filmic and the digital image, which exist in vital tension with the body's own disintegration and disappearance within urban space: while film falls through corporeal and urban matter, recording and transforming its images of the body and the city as it descends, the digital image is contrarily engaged in an ascendant, corporate delirium around the body, focusing on its multiple subjugations. The city's surfaces form the site for that visual divergence around the body: a conflict won from its first moment by the digital image's ostensibly unassailable media supremacy. The digital image and the film image proceed too at disparate rates of erosion in their rapport with the body: the digital image evanesces instantly, but operates through infinite replacement, while the film image's integral process of decay parallels that of the human body's own substance. Caught in that crucial disparity, the city's inhabitants undergo visual dilemmas and contradictions that generate a propulsive sense of pure aberration, which renders them capable of oblivious survival through all of the city's media variants and episodic mutations.

Those urban contradictions are embodied in the imageries of directors working simultaneously in film and digital media at a moment when a boundary between the two is still discernible and tangible to some degree. John Maybury's work shifts between narrative films and experiments in digital media, his preoccupations anchored in the body and the city. The oblivion accorded its inhabitants by the city's exhaustive visual dilemmas is also pivotal to Maybury's filmic and digital images, which attempt to unearth traces of memory in the space between the two media. In Maybury's film on the nature of memory within the digital city, *Remembrance of Things Fast*, only the most fragile splinters of memory (the memory of sex, pre-eminently) can be extracted, against the grain, from the city's engulfing media layers. However, in his 1998 narrative film around the relationship in 1960s London between the painter Francis Bacon and his lover George Dyer, *Love is the Devil*, Maybury constrains the role of the digital to encapsulating the explosions of paint thrown by Bacon at his canvases; the digital is made to carry the gestural, archaic resonances of those creative acts. Maybury's excavation of the corporeal and sensory material of memory, accessible at the volatile margin between the filmic and the digital, is conducted with a rigorous control of its contrary components. In the work of the Holland-based director Ian Kerkhof, that probing of the disappearing ground between the filmic and the digital goes rapidly awry. The digital image, even more than the film image, exacts an inflexible structure of narrational homogeneity for itself, as in *Amsterdam Wasted* (1997). Only in Kerkhof's experiments with urban soundscapes and the digital image, such as his documentary about the Japanese musician Masami Akita, *Merzbow* (1998), is that movement into homogeneity shattered.

Memory generates the central frailty around which all images, of all media, collapse. Both films and digital media scan and carry the intricate metamorphoses that extend from history to image, from city to image and from body to image; memory tenaciously adheres those visual movements together, but also imbues them with the element of dissolution that finally compacts the very first images of urban cinema (Le Prince's film of Leeds Bridge) with the most contemporary digital image of the city. The film historian Paolo Cherchi Usai has charted the course of that dissolution, provoked and sustained by memory:

> Travel, leisure, hilarious or notable occurrences are at the origins of the moving image. More precisely, moving images arise out of an intent to transform into an object whatever is forgettable and therefore doomed to decay and oblivion. The impermanence of these events finds its empirical counterpart in the moving image and determines its status as an artifact.[1]

All the way from the most immediate digital image, reversing backwards in time to the origins of the city-film image in ambitions of technological innovation or popular entertainment, memory and the intimation of death perpetually override the urban image's aims in both art and commerce: to astonish, to captivate and to project an unprecedented style or sensory impact at the body of its spectator.

In multimedia performance art, especially in Japan, the forced confrontation of digital with filmic images works to manifest the inscription and effacement of history on the human body in the city. In the work of the Japanese artist Shinjin Shimizu, that intensive rapport, mediated by film, collides with digital images of the city's contemporary corporate surfaces. Shimizu employs archival film of Japan's seminal, often concealed conflicts – images of its brutal military invasions of the 1930s together with images from late-'60s footage of the suppressed Shinjuku riots – as a primary medium to interrogate and negate the city's contemporary matter: its omnipresent digital media and its subjugated urban bodies. In recent projects, Jean-Luc Godard has also employed the strategic juxtaposition of historically charged film footage with digital media in order to assemble an exploration of the visual image's power and infirmity: his short film *On the Origin of the Twenty-First Century* (2000) forms a caustic revelation of the contemporary moment through the fracturing of digital images by invocatory sequences of film images of the twentieth century's defining atrocities and power struggles.

Although the digital and the filmic have been viewed by many visual artists as existing in hostile interaction, aligned at variance over disputed urban and corporeal terrains, their imageries possess a dual, allied vulnerability to the forces of memory and oblivion, and to the arbitrariness of corporate culture. In the contemporary city, the fragile seams of images at the raw juncture between the filmic and the digital constitute areas at which the body's forms and sensory resonances may be illuminated with an ephemerality or endurance that hinges above all on the survival or obliteration of the traces of cinema, and on the exigencies that transact and annul the city's digital zones.

Malfunction is the driving element of the contemporary city. An integral breakdown in the city's media screens comprises the pre-eminent experience of all journeys across Europe's visual landscapes. Even the essential arrangement of urban space constitutes a cracked matter within which the city is at variance with itself. The web of digital culture extends from the city's centre to its corporate annexes: the sprawling business parks, with their multiplex complexes, that increasingly constellate its suburbs. Beyond those visually regulated sectors, with their intricate susceptibility to malfunction, the city's peripheral swathes are excluded from, or else oppose, its digital seizure; any disused or damaged corporate screen in those areas often appears to have been illuminated in the first place. The city's peripheral terrains remain under the visual sway of cinema rather than that of the digital image; those urban spaces were exhaustively surveyed across a century by cinema, so that the city's malfunctioning slippage into and out of its peripheries became uniquely known and perceived via filmic images – the disorientating transit from the peripheries to the core (minutely tracked in films from every decade of cinema, for instance *Berlin Alexanderplatz* and *Bicycle Thieves*) is vitally engrained in film. The city's peripheral areas form shut-down spaces for their inhabitants, who themselves embody a fundamental dysfunction of the power of the digital city and its corporate imageries.

Although film often appears to be an endangered and even extinct medium, from the perspective of journeys across incandescent cities within which cinema spaces comprise ramshackle or utterly vanished presences, it is the digital image whose form remains perpetually poised for extinguishment. At every moment, the imminence of a seminal digital crash is ready to obliterate the city's corporate media, encompassing their visual and corporeal manifestations and leaving nothing behind. By contrast, the malfunction of cinema constitutes only a momentary celluloid tear, which provides the sensory relief of a blank interval to the inhabitants of multiply ignited urban surfaces. Especially in such spaces as Europe's disappearing martial-arts and pornography cinemas, where that rip in the matter of celluloid structures the film's screening as habitually as manual blows and sexual acts, such an image-less interval gives its vocal spectators the last-ditch opportunity to elatedly berate an obsolete technology and its hapless operators (an opportunity fundamentally denied to all interrogators of urban digital screens, despite those surfaces' own relentlessly enacted obsolescence). The urban film image, torn again and again, also acquires an indispensable texture of erasure and the addition of new, aberrant layers to the image of the city that it projects.

In addition to their self-generated capacity for malfunction, the city's digital media are also exposed to potential eruptions of human intervention, exacted directly upon urban visual surfaces. In such insurgent approaches, stimulated by ecological or anti-corporate concerns, a primary visual source lies in film images of urban uproar, such as the footage of late-'60s Tokyo and the Paris of May 1968, where virulently inscribed graffiti saturate the city's cancelled commercial hoardings. Alongside those filmic provocations, one inspirational human figure for such forms of media insurgency (and a prescient assailant, in the long-gone era of mid-'70s terrestrial television, of the dynamics of digital culture) may be that of Elvis Presley, who regularly used a handgun to shoot and explode the screen of his television sets whenever the slightest degree of dissatisfaction or lassitude, induced by that screen, demanded a violent retort. The fulfilment of Presley's visual desires required the immediate, repeated replacement of the destroyed medium rather than of the negligible image itself – his Graceland lackeys always had ready a new, pristine television set to manoeuvre into his line of fire, replacing the screen that had been detonated. In the contemporary city, all urban surfaces remain uniquely open to abrupt insurgencies of disabused, un-hypnotized violence: the ricochets of such strategies of human intervention, proliferating from surface to surface, engender the vulnerability for corporate media of an unending visual calamity, as potentially irreparable as the implications of a fatal digital malfunction.

The contemporary city often exerts its own impacts at their maximal intensity at night, from its clogged avenues and luminescent image-screens, precipitating a comprehensive sensory malfunctioning of its visually engulfed inhabitants – a strategy that serves to counter and dilute the potential assaults which any dissident spectator of digital culture might attempt to inflict on those screens. In its most headlong state of operation, the digital city holds the capacity to induce an ocular black-out on the part of its aggrieved inhabitants, along with a compulsory suppression of vision. In its most acute instance, such a shutdown may generate a terminal urban malfunction, transmitted directly from the city to the neurally overloaded corporeal limits of its inhabitants. In such an urban psychosis, the city maintains its unassailable corporate magnitude and can never be subjected to disintegration from the outside; instead, the overturned sensory and visual faculties of its inhabitants are sent reeling, all digital and filmic images irreversibly scrambled together in that perception and scattered at random across the city's oblivious face.

Although the multiple forms of digital malfunction constitute the urgent dilemmas of the contemporary city, both in Europe and Japan, film too has always malfunctioned in its rapport with urban space. Film, throughout its history, intimated to the city the overriding presences of death, memory and dissolution layered within its grandiose urban forms; more directly, at moments of social upheaval, it unsettled the streets of the city and provoked fissures in its power structures, comprising the pre-eminent visual medium for revolutionary or oppositional preoccupations whose ultimate zone of operation was urban space itself. On a more delicate level, film explored raw nuances of the sensations of urban disintegration which are inaccessible to the digital image. In its resistant and tenacious approach to urban space and time, film constituted a vital, creative malfunction of the city.

The rapport between the digital city and the human body inflects every image transmitted from its media screens, and envelops too the past and future existence of film within urban space. Even in its most visually spectacular forms, the contemporary city still emanates its dependence on the presence of its inhabitants, with their physical and visual engagement with its apparitions. That spectatorial captivation pivots on the necessary sustaining of the momentary adherences to the digital image of the city's inhabitants, just as film cities had their axis in the corporeal engagement of their cinema audiences, whose sensory concentration on the image of the city habituated itself to being transferred across the boundary from the cinema space into exterior urban space itself. However, the spectators of the digital city are constituted solely as the objectives of its ocular subjugation, comprising both the primary content and the audience of the city's corporate screens. The unique, corporeal urban matter of those spectators stands in antithesis – as a justifying, contrary element – to the unending evanescence of the city's media images. The body also serves as the essential source of movement for those urban screens, since the digital image must encompass all of the conflicting caprices, styles and deviations of corporeal gesture, in order not to lapse into the terminal stasis of void repetition which is its default mode. But this entails a filtering into the digital of the body's insurgence: the corporeal forms a crucial, but also disruptive and corrupting, compulsion for images of the contemporary city.

Once the city's digital and corporeal elements have meshed, as a corrupt but dominating amalgam, they disseminate an infinitely mutating arrangement of visual and physical traces that fires the city's screens and surfaces; since media systems function through obsessive accumulation, via the relentless overstatement and multiplication of images and information, the body itself proliferates throughout the city, generating uneasy, abrasive relations between the projections of digital media and the urban spaces on which those media exert themselves. The city's filmic image possessed the capacity to move simultaneously in every temporal direction; the under-pinning exigency of the digital city is to forcibly seize its own contemporary moment. However, the contemporary moment forms an awry, ambivalent element within digital culture, which veers wildly from technological archaism to visual redundancy between each of its projections of the corporate body; on jour-neys around Europe and Japan, it often appears as though the contemporary moment is setting out to elude the digital city, with its contamination of the physical and homogenization of urban deviance, and that it is deriding, even negating, the idea of a 'digital culture'.

The contemporary city strategically accords its own system of eminence to its media; above the space of the city and the eyes of its inhabitants, the relentless elevation of illumi-nated corporate insignia, and of sanctioned images of the body, prioritises those overarching visual components of the urban arena. The film image employed a divergent approach to the imprinting of its concerns on the city's face. For many decades, the alluring bodies of film stars were postered over disused urban façades, their forms extending in undifferentiated swathes from the city's centre to the peripheries; the figure of Ricci in *Bicycle Thieves*, miraculously touching the body of Rita Hayworth on the fabulous poster image that his gestures have materialized on the city's shabby surface, intimates the way in which film could conjure the tangible presence of living flesh within the city and mediate it directly from resonant images to the senses of the city's inhabitants and its cinema spectators. The digital city manifests a more skeletal, dissolving physical content, too desiccated and ephemeral for human vision to securely attach itself to; the city's image-screens relentlessly exclaim their transitory inhabitation by anonymous, corporately engendered bodies. Even in film's dereliction, it still contrarily infuses itself into the seminal images of the urban body.

The anomalous revelation that emerges from within the digital city and becomes projected outwards to the gaze of its inhabitants is contained in the way in which that city's volatile juxtaposition of visual and corporeal elements serves to un-screen the essential dilemmas of the human body. In the sudden disappearances and annulments of its digital images, the city unwillingly exposes zones of memory, disintegration and erasure, all of which have an impact on the presence of the human body within urban space. The city's inhabitants also hold the active potential, sustained by film images of historical parallels in the forms of riots and protests, to conduct their own innovative or furious experiments of the body against the city, creating aberrant visions through their capacity to exact sensory transformations. But at the same time as the digital city provokes such corporeal revelations and upheavals, it also relentlessly exerts its own saturating corporate pacification, so that its imageries of the body are finally hinged between the comatose and the insurgent.

With the capricious intervention of one fundamental technological mishap, only the body would remain in the city, excised from the digital and still gesturing in fury or ecstasy at the city's emptied-out image-screens. That vanished intimacy of the digital and the corporeal would necessarily generate entirely new urban forms, of the kind that film alone – across its vast history of envisaging flawed or devastated cities – possessed the ability to explore and visualize. The future in urban space of both the film and the digital image lies in the endurance of the human body as their vital medium.

Cinema possesses its institutionally designated survival zones, both within and beyond urban space, in the contrary forms of film archives and of digital archives of film, although that archival preservation of cinema – and of its images of the city and the body – carries its own system of instability, which interconnects with the vanishing spaces of cinema in the city itself. Over the second half of the twentieth century, the film archive existed in intimate parallel with the archive of the book (although prior to the work of Henri Langlois and the creation of the Cinémathèque Française, few people considered that film was a medium worth conserving at all), and this crucial proximity subsists in digital archives of image and text. The exposure and concealment of the gestural, corporeal traces of writing and of the visual, urban traces of film-making constitute similar processes within the encompassing form of the digital archive. Both the media of the book and the film hold their intricate contents of history and memory, and their conservation over the final decades of the twentieth century functioned through an equivalent accumulation of materials, often unselectively gathered (that element of all-inclusiveness being the central trait of Langlois' work). At its origin, the image of the archive itself, its space visualized in its pre-digital form, was one of untold gatherings of material, with chaotic proliferations of paper or celluloid expanding infinitely across that space; all attempts on the part of an investigator of images or texts to 'find' their desired material became subject both to the engrained idiosyncrasies of such institutions and to the elusiveness of that material's historical and corporeal presences, with archives functioning like hostile cities, always ready to evade their inhabitants' determined ocular and tactile intrusions.

The digital archive holds all images, and all bodies and cities, within itself; its visual manifestation within the space of the city is pre-eminently that of Tokyo's digital-media archive, the NTT Intercommunication Center, opened in 1997 and housed on one storey of an immense corporate and cultural tower in the impenetrable district of western Shinjuku. In that inexhaustible archive, whose user is instantly overwhelmed by more digital images gathered in a moment than the eye could scan in a lifetime, a scattering of computer screens is arranged around the otherwise bare room (although the archive's prohibitive nature and atmosphere, at least, remain intact in that space from its former manifestation). The visual and textual material is accumulated solely into those computers as a densely miniaturized counterpart to the digital city's corporate image-screens, whose vast, exterior forms transmit their incessantly displaced contents from the avenues and urban complexes surrounding the archival space. As with the previous variant of archival space, the digital archive disseminates itself in a direction at fundamental variance from that of the searching eye and body; that ocular exploration is annulled from its first gaze, and the archive's own content, like that of the city's image-screens, remains void, perpetually elusive.

The digital archive of film exists in unsteady rapport with the city's volatile space. Digital media, from their moment of origin, entail the subsuming of the history of film and of the city, extending from a temporal point before their history begins to one after it ends. But the archival engulfing of film and the city, despite its spatial concentration and seamless temporal hold, remains subject to the same digital crash, and the same insurgencies of urban uproar and oblivion, to which the exterior city is, at all times, exposed. As a result, the digital archive of film holds the capacity for abrupt disappearance that film archives also possessed, in their inflammable celluloid's vulnerability to conflagration and disintegration. The images of the city collected in the digital archive are now boundless, multiplied infinitely at each second (whereas in the archive of the film or of the book, a mere vast proliferation of chaotic material accumulated); but those urban images, despite their strength in numbers, remain inflected and encompassed by the digital city's own potential vanishing. Film itself is caught up within an overarching digital process that functions in a parallel universe from that of film's own unique explorations of sensory nuances and responses, and its excavations of urban and corporeal forms. This book, itself an integrally defective archiving of moments from urban cinema, issues from an interval at which film's aberrant imageries can still be perceived in their full sensory range, as digital media gradually overrule those filmic histories of the city.

In their survival outside of the digital archive, the material flaws of film remain vital in their evocation and emanation of the city's essential layers and textures, which are transmitted only via their urban scars and upheavals. The abrasions and tearings over time of the film image, its celluloid bound together by generations of eroding splices, or (in improvised cinema spaces, such as those of pornographic or experimental film) by Sellotape or even saliva, engender a filmic matter which the digital archive works to flatten out and banalize. A total reinvention or cancellation of the filmic city is involved in that archival act: no simultaneity may exist between the filmic city and the digital one once cinema's urban imageries have been meshed into the city's infinite, undifferentiated digital archives. When that process is accomplished, only fragile, sparse traces of film cities can subsist in the retina of the urban inhabitant or spectator, in the form of warped, afterglow images or as peripheral visions of those disappeared film cities. This book – like the project of the German director Werner Herzog's film *Fata Morgana* (1971) to film mirages in the polluted, debris-strewn deserts of North Africa – comprises an attempt to seize illusory or vanishing images, but, as in Herzog's film, those images often appear already to be irrevocably immersed in a covering of visual and urban refuse.

Ultimately, the contemporary digital archive's contents are those which issue from the sustained dynamics of death and the image; these in turn compelled the medium and history of cinema from its first moments. Those dynamics are irresistibly transposed from the moribund archive of the book and the film to that of the digital image, however insensible the institutional or corporate proprietors of the digital archive may be towards the inbuilt vulnerability to disintegration and annulment of its forms. Any book, film or digital image serves to collect, conceal and finally project the traces of death along with the presences it can assemble of transforming cities and of human bodies.

The contemporary city possesses the potential to erase all memory of the experience of film, which, on any journey across urban Europe and Japan, appears now to be held in peripheral, often derelict cinema spaces or to have mutated entirely within the terrain of multiplex complexes; even so, the digital city's future forms remain interlocked, as images in negative, with the forms of urban cinema. The memory generated by film is engrained pre-eminently in the city's contrary matter and space, in the memory of conflict, of sensory experimentation, of pure banality, of visions of revolution, of corporeal upheavals, and of death and origins. Though immediately elided and revoked through the thrall of digital culture, that memory simultaneously constitutes a vast and resistant body of images.

The sustaining and exacerbation over time of the city's digital forms entail an endless process of the cancellation of its images; the element of innovation in contemporary urban structures is often nullified from the first instant, since the imposition of the city's corporate emanations hinges on varied repetition rather than visual seisms. The city's digital images become affixed momentarily to its encompassing screens and surfaces before making their abrupt transit into the already saturated archives of redundant corporate products, and of bodies that only existed (and appear always to have only existed) in order to represent and mediate those products to urban spectators; the contemporary city perpetuates itself through relentless visual and corporeal curtailments and via systematized neural jolts, provocative of consumption.

All urban media are inflected and thrown askew by the essential intangibility and incongruity of digital culture in the contemporary city, its operations fundamentally not aligned with the city's multiple, intricate histories, and unseizable too in their incessantly annulled visual manifestations. That lack of definition serves to make the digital city a source of exultance and ecstasy, as well as of dispossession and subjugation, those divergent responses triggered by the void flux and contradictions of an urban culture in which the sensations of the body can always be instantaneously reversed. If a cinematic narrative capable of incorporating life in the digital city could still be filmed and projected, against the urban grain, it would certainly proceed via a structure of jump-cut rhythms, aberrant caprices and convulsions; the celluloid of such a film would receive the same striating impacts which the contemporary city exacts upon the exposed perception of its inhabitants. The evanescent digital city remains haunted by the embedded presence of filmic traces within it, and by cinema's historical role as the arena for the mediation and subsequent resolution (often via street uproar or other urban shocks) of seminal divisions – above all, between power and insurgence – in the matter of the city.

The visual form of the digital city is determined by the pervasiveness of imageries from corporate Europe and Japan – especially those of youth cultures – within contemporary urban space, and those imageries move effortlessly between one another, and outwards too (to the cities of China and South-East Asia, above all). Alongside that oscillation between Japan and Europe, the urban imageries of the US, once so dominant within the sensory captivations of cinema, appear largely derelict, only capable of being violently reactivated from the exterior. Though the visual cacophony of Hollywood films (enduringly powerful in industrial terms despite their utter redundancy) still resounds negligibly as vacuous fodder for world-wide multiplex complexes, the imageries of the US appear to have been widely supplanted by the forms of European and Japanese cities in the domains of urban style and architecture, and in the mass, momentary fashions (nothing is more vitally transitory than Japanese fashion, its ephemeral dynamics now increasingly transmitted to European cities) that intermittently activate the city's visual life.

The digital and corporate imageries of the contemporary city, despite their built-in fragilities, relentlessly attune and habituate urban space to their projections, and may now – by a final urban aberration – be the perfect realization of the city. But even such an ultimate state of complicity between image and city opens up an infinite zone of visual conflict, originating in the permanently discordant form of the body, its traces and eruptions inscribed across the entire history of urban cinema.

references

1 the origins of the film city

1 Extracts from films by both Louis Le Prince and the Skladanowsky Brothers have been digitally restored by the animator Charl Lucassen and can be viewed on the website http://web.inter.nl.net/users/anima/pre-cinema/.

2 The account given here as the most probable sequence of events is based on consultations of manuscript letters between Dulac and Artaud, held at the Bibliothèque de l'Arsenal, Paris, and in the archives of Artaud's literary executor Paule Thévenin; on descriptions of the screening in newspapers and magazines of the time, also held at the Bibliothèque de l'Arsenal; and on interviews I conducted in 1986–7 with collaborators of Artaud to whom he had recounted his memories of the events in the mid-1940s.

2 urban space in european cinema

1 Leos Carax, 'Tout ça c'est des mots', *Cahiers du cinéma*, 448 (Supplement) (1991), p. 97. Translation by the author. The documentary referred to is *Guy Debord: Son art et son temps*

(1994), directed by Brigitte Cornand in collaboration with Debord.

3 japan: the image of the city

1 Andrey Tarkovsky, *Time Within Time: The Diaries 1970–1986* (London, 1994), pp. 43–4.
2 Chris Marker, *Le Dépays* (Paris, 1982), unpag. Translation by the author.
3 Donald Richie, *Tokyo* (London, 1999), p. 27.
4 Takahiko Iimura, *60s Experiments* (Paris, 1999), p. 5. This paragraph is also based on my discussions with Iimura in Tokyo.

4 the digital city and cinema

1 Paolo Cherchi Usai, *The Death of Cinema: History, Cultural Memory and the Digital Dark Age* (London, 2001), p. 65.

acknowledgements

I'm grateful for the support and encouragement for this book shown to me by the Sainsbury Centre for Visual Arts, and Professor John Onians; the European Research Centre at Kingston University, and Professor Lieve Spaas; Chris Marker; Donald Richie; and the Japan Foundation, and its Director of Programmes in London, Stephen McEnally.

index